D0922153

The
Happiness
Formula

IQ + EQ + GQ = HQ™

Kasandra Vitacca

3:20 Designs Publishing
An Imprint of SEGR Publishing LLC
2150 W. Northwest Hwy #114-1168
Grapevine, TX, USA 76051
Kasandra Vitacca

Printed in the United States of America
First Printing 2018
First Edition 2018

10 9 8 7 6 5 4 3 2 1

ISBN: 978-1-61920-067-8
Library of Congress
Control Number: 2018966319

Cover design by: Andrea McNeeley
www.320.designs.com

Editor: Heidi Clingen
www.Allwritey.com

"Folks are usually about as happy as they make their minds up to be."
— **Abraham Lincoln**

"Take responsibility of your own happiness, never put it in other people's hands."
— **Roy T. Bennett, *The Light in the Heart***

"Learn to value yourself, which means: fight for your happiness."
— **Ayn Rand**

"I'm happy. Which often looks like crazy."
— **David Henry Hwang, *M. Butterfly***

DEDICATION ♥

The Happiness Formula
Is dedicated to YOU!

_____
(Fill in your name)

As I wrote "The Happiness Formula," I thought of people I
know well,
people I have met along the way,
people I will meet, and
I prayed for ALL of you!
I wrote this book for YOU and
I pray you are blessed by it and, of course,
closer to your HAPPY!

TABLE OF CONTENTS

FOREWORD 1

INSPIRATION FOR "THE HAPPINESS FORMULA" 5

ARE YOU READY TO BE HAPPY? 11

WHAT DOES IT TAKE TO BE HAPPY? 25

WHAT IS "HAPPY"? 32

BARRIER 1: THE LITMUS TEST 40

BARRIER 2: EXPECTATIONS 55

IQ – INTELLECTUAL QUOTIENT 60

EQ – EMOTIONAL QUOTIENT 74

GQ – GOD QUOTIENT 87

CHOOSE WELL 108

YOU TOO HAVE SUPERPOWERS 119

WE ARE SPIRITUAL BEINGS HAVING A HUMAN
EXPERIENCE 126

"THE HAPPINESS FORMULA" PLAYED OUT IN MY
LIFE 137

BE YOUR OWN BEST CASE-STUDY 151

LIVING IN THE TRANSITION, THE GAP, & THE
AWKWARD DISCOMFORT 167

HOW DO YOU "DO" HAPPINESS? 172

IF – RUDYARD KIPLING 175

THF DAILY "TO-DOS" 187

ANNUAL PLANNING 190

HOW THF APPLIES TO HEALTH 203

HOW THF APPLIES TO WEALTH.................................209

HOW THF APPLIES TO RELATIONSHIPS
(MARRIAGE) 214

FINAL THOUGHTS..221

AFTERWORD 229

MY PRAYER STAPLES 231

TRUISMS TOO GOOD NOT TO SHARE 234

MUSIC MAKES MERRY...247

FOREWORD

I first met Kasandra Vitacca when she was introduced to me as someone who might be a candidate for us as a recruiter for our financial services firm. Our first meeting was interesting. Kasandra told me several times that she wasn't interested in a "corporate" job and how she really didn't want to do this. It was clear though, at some level, she was interested.

Kasandra Vitacca Mitchell is a force of nature. As you will learn in the pages ahead, she is passionate about her beliefs, she is highly intelligent, and she is vocal about her positions. She is an engaging extrovert who easily fills a room with her laughter and strength. I remember thinking she would be a great recruiter. It turns out she was much more.

To be a great recruiter, you must be able to paint a picture and create a vision to inspire the candidate. You must be able to create empathy and relatability and build a real bond with the candidate to be effective. You also must also do a lot of networking and relationship building to find the type of candidates who might be able to do the work we do at our firm. It is highly entrepreneurial and requires being able to process at a very high intellectual level given the nature of the planning we do.

In that first meeting, I could tell Kasandra Vitacca Mitchell not only had the entrepreneurial drive and the higher order thinking ability needed to do the job, she had the people skills to really make it work. What wasn't apparent in that first

1

meeting was the depth of her passion to really want to serve and help people.

As we worked together and began meeting and interviewing potential candidates for our firm, I began to see the fire in Kasandra to want to really do something to help people. Financial issues are the leading cause of divorce and unhappiness in America. As she learned our process and became a client herself, Kasandra began to become interested in working as a representative. In less than three years, Kasandra Vitacca Mitchell rose to become one of the leading advisors in the nation.

Over the years, I was privileged to watch Kasandra grow and mature not just as a representative, but as a person. It has been exciting and interesting to see her desire to serve turn into her writing this book. It is timely and needed in this crazy world in which we live.

The book you are about to read is really a "How To" for living life. Proverbs 21:31 says "The horse is prepared for the day of battle, but victory is of the Lord". This is easily one of my favorite guiding principles. However, it doesn't really tell us how to prepare. This book will be a huge help in learning how to live.

As a teenager, my Mom used to tell me that "Happiness isn't a destination, it's a by-product of the journey". Kasandra Vitacca Mitchell teaches how to walk this journey. It is a mindful, step by step approach to understand happiness and enjoy happiness as we go through this journey of life.

Despite hardship, setbacks, inconveniences, failures, we can still be happy. Kasandra Vitacca Mitchell lays out the formula and it is truly inspiring.

Joseph Kane

Founder, Personal Economics Group

Kasandra Vitacca

INSPIRATION FOR
"THE HAPPINESS FORMULA™"

So much of who I am and what shaped how I saw the world and its people was a product of what I learned from my mother. She was my world growing up! In hindsight, she was my "god." She was and remains a great mother. Even as I openly speak of her "mistakes" and the ways she taught me, ideas and belief systems I did not pass on to my son, as I age I become more aware of her undeniable excellence, downright brilliance, and unconditional love.

While I have not continued some of my mother's thought patterns and life philosophies, I am indebted to what she wanted for me. She wanted me to be completely self-sufficient with skills and knowledge that would allow me to do anything, be anything, go anywhere and experience all life has to offer. She did not want me tied down such that I could not explore. She did not want me hindered in any way such that I could not experience. My mother wanted me to have it ALL and, alas, she did it. I have a life beyond my wildest dreams. I have a life that is extraordinary, and I am very clear it is not an easy life for the uber-majority to attain. I am not just blessed; I am abundant! I AM HAPPY.

Mom, you are fantastic!

So what did mom teach me? Bear in mind, she may not hold some of these thoughts anymore, but as I reflect upon the direct messages of her words and all the indirect and more powerful messages of her actions, the following is what I learned in no particular order:

- She taught me to never rely on a man.
- She taught me to forget marriage because monogamy was a myth.
- She taught me to ignore religion because the institution is paternalistic and misogynistic.
- She taught me never to let them see you cry.

- She taught me to suck it up because someone always has it worse.
- She taught me always to smile because you never know who needs a kind face.
- She taught me to be a student at all times so I should always ask questions, always seek knowledge, always humble myself enough to admit, at least to myself, "I could be wrong" or, even if I am "right," there might be even more to know. Remember, good is the enemy of great.
- She taught me to seek excellence always. Coming in 2nd place is fine, as long as you fought hard for 1st.
- She taught me to play hard, to never quit, to push myself until I puke.
- She taught me to practice hard and with the intensity I would bring to the game because how you practice is how you play…and winning matters!
- She taught me to say "I am sorry" by modeling it herself.
- She taught me that people make mistakes and you can love them anyway. "There but for the Grace of God go I," was her most oft-quoted life lesson and it remains one of my favorites.
- She taught me to respect the janitor just as much as the principal.
- She taught me to care about my body, my health, my mind by engaging in a physical exercise, sports, daily activity.

Some of what my mom taught me, I still practice, and some I am 180 degrees from what she espoused. I also learned by watching. Yes, parents, we teach our children (and others) more about what we value, what we believe, by our actions than by our words. As such, I learned a lot of what NOT to do largely by how we lived. I was able to see the consequences of my mother's actions and often inaction, and I wanted something different for my life.

"Your actions speak so loudly, I cannot hear what you are saying."
--Ralph Waldo Emerson

Many months after I wrote this extemporaneous free-flow of thoughts in early June 2018, I stopped journaling. I forgot I had thought about writing a book until I went on a 4-day silent retreat at the end of July 2018. The day after my return my husband and I did what we do every morning: we sit for 60-90 minutes drinking coffee, sharing stories, encouraging each other. During our time "The Happiness Formula"™ was born!

For a couple of years, I had been writing about and giving presentations with the IQ (intellectual quotient) and EQ (emotional quotient) elements clearly stated, but I was more clandestine about GQ (god quotient™). I give most of my presentations in secular settings; you can't just start talking about God and hope people won't freak out. I also had my concerns. I was raised in a non-Christian, nonreligious, "our brain and what we control is our god" home. (Reference back to the list of some of what I learned growing up.) As such, my trepidation to include "god" as a key variable to happiness is a risk.

Further, no matter what principles created the foundation of the United States, this country is NOT a "God-fearing" nation. We are so far removed from our Judeo-Christian roots that the one group with whom it is acceptable to harangue is the group that calls itself "Christian." Another example is Caucasian males. Simply by their skin tone and genitalia, they are categorized. Some people blame that category for many of the problems with our society. Add the word "Christian" to white males, and another category is created. Some people claim this category of people is "privileged" and therefore less capable of understanding people from other categories.[1] But that's another book.

As for this book, on July 23, 2018, I knew I wanted to write a book that was explicit in what will create the peace, joy, freedom – HAPPINESS – we all seek:

(1) think, learn, get educated – it's a function of IQ (reality)
(2) act, apply what you have learned, honestly assess your feelings and make a decision – it's a function of EQ (application)
(3) align, you are what you feed your mind, choose a God and walk the path – it's a function of GQ (possibility)

"The Happiness Formula" does not attempt to apologize for asserting without reservation or hesitation that you will NOT attain the highest level of happiness (peace, joy, freedom, success, satisfaction, comfort, love, all things good and wonderful), if you do not invite God into the equation of your

---

[1] On the off chance you believe I personally feel this way, I pray you read that with the facetious intent with which it was meant. I want to make a point without getting too deep into a topic for which I cannot expand in this book and, yet, it is this type of thinking which keeps so many people away from the highest quotient of happiness.

life. Yes, you must educate yourself and never stop learning; IQ matters. Yes, you must work even harder to control your emotions and respond rather than react because research proves EQ is THE #1 reason people rise to the highest leadership ranks across all industries and fields. Therefore, EQ matters more! But, people who have a specific God they can name and a god-system they can follow, are happier. GQ matters most!

And yet no one says all of this in one book. Why don't we combine all three of these elements – our intellect, our emotions, our spirit – as we examine how to improve, enhance, elevate our wealth, health, personal relations, careers...happiness?! We have been brainwashed with the separation of church and state; we believe it is not possible to live in a way that honors ALL of ourselves. Hence, we are not happy.

"The Happiness Formula" seeks to put all three together – IQ + EQ + GQ – because when you apply all three elements to all areas of your life, your HQ (happiness quotient™) will inevitably increase! The purpose of "The Happiness Formula" is to bring you to an awareness that as you work on your mind (IQ) and grow in maturity (EQ) while covering all your efforts in the mantle of your God (GQ), your quotient of "happy" will be as high as possible, which, in my experience, seems to be exponential!

ARE YOU READY TO BE HAPPY?

Everyone wants to be happy so isn't this book meant for everyone? Not really.

The truth is, most people don't begin to explore this question at a level that will make a difference until they have that good old "mid-life crisis." It isn't until someone has either had a minor breakdown, a momentary depression or even a major crash, that s/he begins to examine this question deeply enough, long enough, with enough honestly and humility, to do anything. And, even then, the formula to happiness will not be understood by everyone.

The quest for peace, joy, freedom – happiness – takes work. As such, "The Happiness Formula" is for those who want an A, people who have a competitive spirit with whom their main competition is themselves. "The Happiness Formula" is for leaders, whether one leads only her/himself or a team of thousands. It is for the person for whom "good is the enemy of great." It is for those who want more and are willing to do what it takes. It is for those who don't mind the sweat and tears and pain and struggle. It is for those who enjoy the work out almost as much as the victory and, to some extent, they already comprehend the Truth – the victory, the joy, the HAPPY, is IN the process.

"The Happiness Formula" is not just about visualizing yourself as a winner – standing on the podium with the award, receiving the memorandum of understanding because you have won the contract, fitting into the dress you wore 20 years ago – it is in working towards your goal and engaging in the process of excellence, you find your freedom, your peace, your HAPPY!

If you are too young, you certainly have not had a mid-life crisis although you might have had some trauma. You may even be a "type A" personality who seeks excellence in all you do. In general though, the quest for "happiness" may not resonate as deeply with a person who is still in the phase of life where you are just trying to figure out what it means to truly be on your own.

Case in point, I was 28 years old and in my second full-time career after college graduation, because this new industry paid twice as much as the career I had just left. An "old person" (he was in his early 50s) was a contractor at my company, a job title I was unclear about, so I began to ask questions. To this day, I remember him saying what "old" people always say, "Money is not everything." He added some statements about having enough to pick and choose his jobs, which is why he was a contractor rather than a W2 employee, and other trite statements that made no sense to a young woman who knew in the recesses of her young heart that title and money mattered, and she wanted more!

Thus, my response, "I think you are either blowing smoke up my butt or trying to convince yourself you have done well because that platitude means nothing to me. When I get to where you are, I will let you know what I believe about what you are saying now." While my words may have been a bit softer, there is a high probability they were not. I detested "old" people telling me money wasn't everything when I listened to them lament and watched them struggle and worry. If money isn't everything, then to my 20-something mind, "old" people should be a lot happier about the money they had considering it was a lot more than my income.

Then there is the phase where you settle in a bit. Maybe you have a steady partner or even a spouse. Maybe you have children or are in the process of planning for kids. More importantly, people who enter this "second phase of adulthood" have begun to live in the realities of "adulting" long enough to realize they do not know enough. For some, their ego and bravado will keep them from seeking advice while the majority of others will look for answers but they will only research so much. They will rely heavily on parents or "elders" they believe to be more successful without digging deeper into the truths and facts. The reality is, this phase of adulthood, when you have taken on the care of others, usually finds one with so much on their plate – significant others, young children, job pressures, changing body challenges, shifting friend dynamics, etc. – you simply have not figured out how to slow down long enough to assess what is happening.

"The Happiness Formula" will resonate deepest with a "seasoned" adult. The key is, a seasoned adult has been in the workforce long enough to know "all that glitters is not gold." She has already been laid off, quit, or been fired. She has moved houses and even states. She has discovered that all the money she put into her 401K or outside IRA is not much more than the amount she contributed over time and the real estate property she invested in that she thought was going to make her a millionaire overnight is more of a headache to manage than the money she earns from it. And the weight begins to show on the hips and in the stomach, along with aches and pains one had heretofore not known.

Even more fundamentally, by the time someone is "seasoned," the bravado of youth has been tamed. The dreams of glory have been subdued. The hopes of greatness have been tempered. And, the deaths begin. Friends don't make it to your 20-year class reunion and even fewer by your 30th. A parent or a close relative has died and usually several. Even children do not always outlive parents. By "mid-life," one's mortality begins to take hold, and the questions of purpose, value, worth, impact and why you exist in the first place begin to get louder and louder in your head. Thus, by mid-life one begins to say more consistently, "I just want to be happy. I want my kids to be happy."

So the question becomes, is this it?! Is this what the second half of my existence will look like?! Is life about the day-in-day-out monotony where I feel like I am going nowhere? Is "Groundhog Day" real? Is it possible to skip and dance one's way into eternity or does life just stink and then you die? After all, I think some people might actually to be happy, joyous, and free ... not that I know a lot of them, but so many people seem to be happy – but are they? And, if they are, what do they know? What have they learned that I missed somehow?

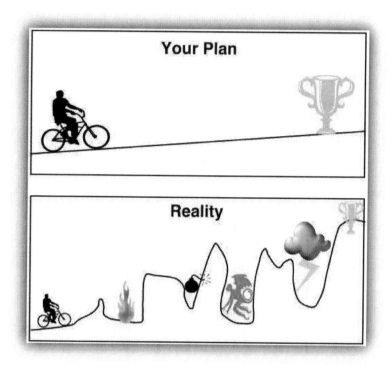

Hence, the "mid-life crisis" begins. Couples grow more distant and turn to the temporary revelry of the periodic "girls night out" or "what happens in Vegas stays in Vegas" lifestyle. Alcohol, drugs, and porn become staples such that one becomes desensitized to the amount and frequency of their use. Or, couples try to stay together by going to church more or paying for counseling or they attend spouse-swapping parties. Some have secret affairs while others get divorced. Men buy fancier cars and take more risk with their investments only to lament, "I can make millions. But I can't keep it." Women seek answers in their appearance as they inject poisons into their face and cut off other parts or they simply give in to the difficulties of staying slim, so they go the other route and engorge themselves.

We don't see as well. We don't heal as fast. Our bodies change noticeably. We do not have the money we dreamed of having nor the relationships we had hoped to have. We attend a lot more funerals. Aging is NOT for the weak, which is why so many stop trying.

Health, Wealth, and Relationships are THE areas that cause the majority of our discomfort, disease, and unhappiness. You can listen to all the expert advisors, read all the self-help, and study all the gurus, but for about 67% of the American populace[1], happiness is elusive and seemingly unattainable. There is a solution, but it takes time, work, patience, hope, faith, and surrender. It works for those who want an A, whose main competition is themselves, and who know "good is the enemy of great."

"The Happiness Formula" is for those who have not given up. It works best for the seasoned adult who has put in the effort to get healthier, wealthier and wise even if they have yet to attain the outcome they desire or reach the coveted state of continual happiness. It is for those who seek and believe they will find because they have faith they are destined for greatness. It is the mindset of a leader which enables one to gain happiness. This leader, however, is "special" insofar as she has the unique combination of honesty with self and others, willingness to re-learn that which she thought she already knew, fortitude to stay the course especially when it feels too hard or seems unclear, and, fundamentally, s/he has humility and hope.

---

[1] "...only 33% of Americans surveyed said they were happy. In 2016, just 31% of Americans reported the same. Americans have never been the happiest bunch, Gerzema says. In the nine-year history of the happiness poll, the highest happiness index was 35% in 2008 and 2009." http://time.com/4871720/how-happy-are-americans/ July 26, 2017

In the end, this is a "serious" book.

"Happy" can imply balloons and bubbles and giggling and spontaneity but that is exactly what sabotages one's ability to live in a state of sustainable happiness. It's too euphoric and temporal. This book appeals to those who want excellence for themselves, the leader who understands and is okay with the need to think and act like an adult. They simply cannot figure out how to get back to the heart of a child.

But how does one do that? Self-help books don't help. Meditation and yoga don't help. Praying to God and working extra hard don't seem to be enough. So, I try even harder and hire a life coach, join a success group, create a vision board, spend a lot of time "thinking" so that I can "grow rich" by the "law of attraction" – but none of it seems to get me where I need to go and want to be.

What is the ONE thing that will propel me to the success I want and, ultimately, the happiness I desire? Isn't there something that will make a difference?! Isn't there a magic formula that will take care of everything?!

That's why I wrote "The Happiness Formula." We live in a world of data, facts, and stats. But what is the right answer, the correct combination of attitudes, and actions that will make my life the life I have always wanted? We all want health, wealth, peace and prosperity so how do you DO it? How do you GET these wants and needs met without having to become a personal fitness professional or nutritionist, a marriage counselor or a priest, a TV personality or acquire more degrees, work more hours, forgo more of the foods you love, and abstain from TV, sex, alcohol, and, ultimately, pleasure!?

After all, isn't part of being happy about those things which please me? Many of the techniques to get physically or emotionally fit or increase financial or relational wealth, are solutions about self-denial, sacrifice, and giving up what is pleasurable. That does not sound like happiness! Or, the answers are simply too fluffy, too touchy-feely and, in the end, I am left in defeat knowing I cannot muster enough "release of self" and "surrender of wants" to just feel good!

I just want to be happy! I want my kids to be happy. I don't want a lot. I just want those I love to be happy! Is that too much to ask?!

Some people live abundantly happy, healthy and fulfilled lives. However, research proves[1] they seem to be the exception rather than the rule; but they exist. So, what do they know? What do they do?!

I have been asking these questions and researching the answers since I was in elementary school. I was labeled a precocious child from a "broken" home in a struggling, blue-collar suburb of L.A. Early on, school officials identified me with a high intellect. The scores revealed I had "genius" level IQ and I attended a special school for "mentally-gifted minds." While I was studying at the graduate school level and impressing teachers with my intellectual acumen, I was also breaking into people's homes.

---

[1] Ibid.

My goal was not to steal anything; I wanted to learn how people lived – what they valued and believed based on how they organized themselves. What did they eat? How clean were they? Did they have family pictures on display or cheap art or nothing? Did they read non-fiction books or popular culture magazines or Playboy? Did they leave clothes on the floor and dishes in the sink? Did they make their beds?

Studying people convinced me to become a social scientist as I believed if I could understand why and how people make decisions, I could help them avoid thought processes that would lead to their downfall and, as such, I could help them course correct if necessary.

I got a full ride to Stanford for both my Bachelors and Masters and took my first full-time job as a high school teacher of U.S. and World History and Economics and coached volleyball. After a couple of years, I transitioned into adult development and spent the next 12+ years working for corporations, professional member associations, and universities as an "Organizational Design and Efficiency Expert." It was during this time of designing systems to meet the micro-needs and wants of people within the macro framework of an organization's needs and goals, that I refined my skills and talents as a strategic long-term thinker and planner who can help others actualize their greater vision into their immediate, day-to-day reality.

It was during this tenure as a "change agent" that I realized the biggest fear that undermines marriages, destroys health, and robs one of joy, is financial insecurity. Research proves the most intimate conversation you can have with someone is not about their sex life, but rather, how they manage their money. While I did not actively choose to educate people about money, life events would compel me to leave corporate America and become an independent financial advisor.

Transitioning in the world of financial services was a simple process in that the bar is set very low for entry. The industry is set up to reward the best salespeople, not the most educated, nor the most generous. If you like the advisor and trust this person, that is the criteria for making six figures in financial services. "No one cares how much you know until they know how much you care."

While my financial service colleagues have just thrown this book across the room with such a disclosure, those who really can make a difference for others have continued reading. The reality is, the advisor is not to blame for the fact that the uber-majority will spend thousands of dollars in fees and even more in lost time and peace of mind and still end up with nothing or close to nothing. When you consider it is YOUR money, when you consider that no one is going to guarantee your future but YOU, who is ultimately responsible for your financial health? It's like blaming a fitness professional because you pay him $150/hour and yet you are still 100 lbs overweight because you refuse to change your diet and, yet about 90% of your health is what you put into your body.

When I became a financial advisor, I would tell people "I am a fitness professional for finances because I will teach you what you need to do to get financially healthy, but you need to do the work." Thus, a saying I coined, "Money is not math. Money is human behavior."

"money is not math; money is human behaviour."

www.kasandravitacca.com

In 2008, I entered the world of financial services to be what I had always been, an educator. As a teacher at heart, I wanted to give away knowledge I had learned and research, data, insight, and wisdom I had gleaned such that one would no longer need to worry about money. The decisions many people make often are not logical or rational. For them, the quest for happiness will remain a distant vision until they are willing to get educated (IQ), apply what they learned (EQ), and leave the results up to God. (GQ)

"The Happiness Formula" is a book designed for someone who is an adult and ready to experience all the benefits and wisdom and happiness we all had hoped aging would provide without losing the joy of seeing the world through the eyes of a child:

- This book is for the person who is aware that while their Intellectual Quotient (IQ) might be average or even "genius," there is still a lot to learn and s/he is willing to spend some time getting educated. IT IS ABOUT UNDERSTANDING WHAT IS REAL!

- This book is for the person who has a decent enough Emotional Quotient (EQ) such that s/he can quell her ego and listen to advice and implement best practices even when these behaviors might be new or even hard. IT IS ABOUT GAINING A NEW PERSPECTIVE THROUGH NEW ACTIONS!

- This book is for those who want to tap into the Universal Power Source necessary for a peace-filled life. They may have only a mustard seed of faith in God, but their God Quotient™ (GQ) is activated and ready to be increased. IT IS ABOUT ALL THAT IS POSSIBLE!

"The Happiness Formula" is for the person who is ready to have peace, joy, love, and freedom – HAPPINESS – as they apply "The Happiness Formula" to any and every area of their life: IQ + EQ + GQ = HQ™.

<u>WHAT DOES IT TAKE TO BE HAPPY?</u>

There are too many rules, too many lists of what to do to be excellent, successful, healthy, wealthy and wise. "12-steps To This" and "10 Things People Do To Get That" and "7 Easy Ways to Do It All!" If our brains cannot technically process more than one thought at a time and a mature adult can only focus for eight seconds at a time (squirrel!), how the heck can I remember all these rules and checklists especially when they are always so specific? I have to learn the 12 steps for Wealth Building and the 10 To-Dos for Healthy Living and the 7 Easy Ways to Engage Teenagers, and the lists and rules and to-dos go on for every area of my life. It's darn near impossible!

People continue to create more systems of rules which do not bring them the peace, joy, and freedom they truly desire. Happiness is NOT attainable within a system that codifies and qualifies what I should and should not be doing. More often than not, these lists are used to beat us over the head for what we won't or can't do than to help us achieve any semblance of success and, god forbid, happiness.

As such, is there a better way to take all these lists and more appropriately apply them to our own lives? While I might be mature enough to recognize the value of systems and rules and guidelines, is there a more basic way to spur me into "right" living – actions and behaviors that will benefit me and others?

I want a quick checklist that I can process within seconds in my head, in the heat of the moment, to determine if I am making the right decision, saying the right words, choosing the right behavior. I need a tool to help me "by-pass" the part of my brain that first tells me to "fight or flee" (my amygdala) and I need to very quickly process a moment through the more logical part of my brain (my pre-frontal cortex) to ensure I am effective for me and those with whom I interact.

I need something more useful than "take a deep breath and count to 10" or even "Love God first and neighbor second." Those are truths, but they are not practical enough for me. What I have discovered is there are either too many lists with so much meat I cannot digest it all in a way that will allow me to apply it at the moment or, the lists, the systems, the "answers" I have read do not say enough for me to know how even to start. They are too esoteric, too ethereal, too hocus-pocus and "spiritual" to have any real value in a tangible world. I want useful tools I can act upon so that what transpires next (after my nano-second of pause) is more effective for me and others.

"The Happiness Formula"™ will teach you three foundational processes designed to help you filter life's reality and produce a practical outcome, so you will be a more effective and HAPPY person.

1. IQ – What do I know? What information do I have? What factual data and research relates to this moment? What is real? → Engaging our intellect inspires a different set of questions to ask yourself and others.

2. EQ – How do I feel? What emotions are being triggered by this moment? How do I perceive this moment and what other worldviews might exist? → Recognizing your emotions encourages a different level of emotional response so you can respond rather than react.

3. GQ – What else might be happening for all parties involved? Might there be other realities and Truths for which I am not yet ready to be made aware? Is it possible God has a bigger plan in mind? → Filtering everything through a God of your understanding allows for the outcome we all want in the first place – peace, joy, freedom = HAPPINESS.

As I become adept at processing life's moments through "The Happiness Formula," I am better able to respond with the "right" words and actions which will often be very different from what they would have been otherwise. I can admit I do not have enough information and can ask better questions to get at that information. I am more likely to express a concern that might expose a bit of my heart or even allow another to reveal her own more comfortably. I am aware that the world is not all about me and I am more able to maneuver through the moment with maturity and aplomb which allows all parties to get what they want even if "rejection" is part of the outcome. As I become adept at processing life's moments through the formula, IQ+EQ+GQ, I am a much better version of me, and THAT is HQ! (Happiness!)

IQ – searches for the definitions, the data, the facts. Information gathering requires reading and research which are vital to know what options exist. While we do not know everything and do not have time to learn it all, IQ is about what happened in the past. The moment you define something via words, data, facts, stats, definitions, is the moment that information has already passed. It is also why you must never stop learning and why this awareness of the finite limitation of the human intellect is the beginning of humility. If at base you can never know it all, acquire all knowledge, then you are more open to ideas that may counter those which you thought you already knew.

> "The problem in America isn't so much what people don't know; the problem is what people think they know that just ain't so." – Will Rogers

EQ – searches for the connections across the terms with the specific goal to learn what it means for me and others and how we might grow as a result of such exploration and consideration. It is what is real and true at this point, but may not be true tomorrow. It is the ability to flex and maneuver knowing there is so much more to know, explore and feel based on the worldview of others who operate from a perspective 180 degrees from yours. And yet, even with our differences, EQ allows people to take a stand and set boundaries and define what is "real" and "true" for themselves in this present moment. Therefore, EQ is about the present so you can make the best decision possible while accepting one day you may get more data that will cause you to change your mind, and you will. For now, in the present moment, you will do the best you can with the information you have acquired.

"If I'd known better I'd have done better." – Maya Angelou

GQ – searches for the truth so I can evolve towards a better version of myself. I have no control in this because I can only see where I am in the moment. GQ gives me a glimpse of what might be possible in the future. I do not set myself on the path that I have defined, but on the path that Spirit knows in its infinite wisdom. While every decision I make today affects the outcome of my future, I can rest assured, if it were wrong, God would let me know, and I can course correct. And if it was right, I can write a book and share my experience, strength and hope with others!

> "The horse is made ready for the day of battle, but victory rests with the LORD." – Proverbs 21:31 (NIV)

By reading "The Happiness Formula" and putting this thinking, acting, believing process into all areas of your life, you will recognize the unique gift you are and the unique gifts you can offer the world whether that is to impact one person or thousands because the Truth is, to impact one person IS to impact thousands. Thus, do not ever forget, you are ALWAYS a "good" example. You are either a good example of what to do or a good example of what not to do. What sort of gift would you like to offer others?

> "A man's gift makes room for him and brings him before the great." – Proverbs 18:16 (ESV)

A "gift" is an offering. Thus, what you give to the world in and through yourself determines the path you will walk, the doors that will open to you…or not. Is what you offer, are your gifts – your words, your actions, your attitudes – leading down a path towards greatness or something "less than?"

To be happy one must embrace the Truth that Abundant Life if a gift of the Trinity:

IQ – What you can know
EQ – What you can do
GQ – What is possible

When you operate in the fullness of all three elements, you can attain and sustain the highest level of happiness. For centuries people have struggled to understand the Christian Trinity. They asked how can an all-powerful being also be human? And how is the "Holy Spirit" any different than this Omnipotent and Omniscient Entity who already has no physical form? Why is there a need for two "spirits?" If these are the types of arguments that you have presented about the Triune God, again, it might be a challenge for you to accept "The Happiness Formula" because it operates on the same premise. Three seemingly separate realities operate simultaneously.

Neuroscience tells us we only think one thought at a time and yet our brains fire electrical energy in all spheres all at once at almost all times. We are finite beings of limited IQ and able to articulate and define only a micro element, one thought at a time. But we can tap into the mind of the Creator. When you tap into the Spirit, you can see all that has been known and what is possible at the moment. Our Creator in His graciousness may give us a glimpse of the future, but only enough, so we do not miss the trail.

As we tap into The Source and honor our God, it is like a flashlight that hovers above us at all times in the pitch black. It shines its halo toward the future and shows us we are moving in the right, the good, the perfect direction as set for us. When you can see the path forward and you know it is lined with fresh, verdant foliage, you laugh a bit more; you step a bit lighter, you smile. You are happy.

WHAT IS "HAPPY"?

Most adults will recognize the following scene even if the words were a little different when you experienced it:

> Your Friend – "I don't know. I am so tired from working so many hours, but I love my job. My family is healthy, and I would do anything for them, but they are all so different. I feel like I have to be four different personalities if I want to relate. Of course, life is not cheap, and while we are fine financially, there is never enough money for everything we want. I am getting older and…"

> You – "Hey, buddy. Forgive me for cutting in, but you seem to be getting more and more agitated. Take a deep breath. Relax. Answer me this, when you clear away all the demands for your time, your attention, your money, what do you want?"

> Your Friend – "I just want to be happy."

Often your friend, or even yourself, will follow up the "I just want to be happy" statement with something along the lines of, "I don't want to live with any more stress and worry. I don't need to be rich or famous. I just want to be happy."

I mentor juniors and seniors who are part of a leadership development program at a top-ranked university. During our first meeting, I always ask, "What do you want in life?" For several years running, I get a version of this response that came from a more recent mentee of mine, "I want to be happy, have money to support myself and my family, and not struggle. I value being happy and a lifestyle based on people and real relationships. I am big on the simple life, but maybe it's because I can't afford much yet."

These responses are so commonplace that the question arises, "What is happiness?" What does it mean to be happy and why do we juxtapose wealth and fame with happiness? Why is it so common for people to retort upon learning someone has achieved great success, "Good for them, I guess, but are they happy?" Do we assume great success, abundant living (wealth, health, prosperity) are not compatible with happiness? Or, have we begun to accept the subtle and insidious lie that we, me, myself, and I, cannot have both which is why we disbelieve that someone else can "have it all"?

So, again, the question is raised, what is happiness? How does one define "happy"?

When you look at the etymology of the word "happy," it is about being the recipient of good fortune, being favored, and having advantages. All of this pleasure and contentment is from an unknown source. Happy is essentially about being "lucky,"[1] which implies it just happens! How? Why?

---

[1] www.etymonline.com/word/happy. late 14c., "lucky, favored by fortune, being in advantageous circumstances, prosperous;" of events, "turning out well," from hap (n.) "chance, fortune" + -y which is that which allows, fosters or brings about an occurrence
www.dictionary.com/browse/happy?s=t: Fortune = fate, lot, destiny; To be fortunate = having good fortune; receiving good from uncertain or unexpected sources; lucky. Happy: 1. delighted, pleased, or glad, as over a particular thing: to be happy to see a person. 2. Characterized by or indicative of pleasure, contentment, or joy: a happy mood; a happy frame of mind. 3. favored by fortune; fortunate or lucky: a happy, fruitful land.

If we tie happiness to "luck," to a source that is unknown and not definable, we cannot be happy. If we cannot define the source, we won't be able to sustain it. Our HQ will always be low or worse, zero, so, while we cannot precisely articulate what is wrong, we certainly know when we don't "feel" happy. Thus, sometimes, it is easier to define why we are not happy than exactly what will make us happy.

When you look at the opposite of happy, its antonym is sad. To be sad is to experience unhappiness or grief, to be sorrowful or mournful, to be despondent, disconsolate, discouraged, gloomy, downcast, downhearted, depressed, dejected, and melancholy.[1] Just reading that list makes my heart sink a bit. If one is not happy, one is often in a state of downright depression as if someone or something has died!

While this seems a bit extreme and you might argue, "Just because I am not happy does not mean I am depressed and in mourning!" However, the reality is, the reason you are not experiencing joy, cheer, merriment, contentedness, bliss, satisfaction, and your life is not what you would describe as favorable, propitious, successful, and prosperous, (synonyms of happy) is because to be anything other than these is not to be happy and that **is** depressing! Or, at the very least, it feels like something has died – hope, a dream, a longing. We are not happy because something is dead inside of us and so the internal battle begins.

---

[1] www.dictionary.com/browse/sad?s=t

In the deepest recesses of our soul, we scream to be alive. We know that anything less than a joy-filled life, a happy life, is death. We clamor for happiness and begin to fight against the feelings of sadness. Essentially, we scream, "I want to be alive!" but I have no idea how to get there. So we begin to declare "I deserve better!"

It is this fight, this confusion, the unknown, that drives us to change jobs about as many times as we change lovers. While we are not sure exactly what will make us happy, we know what makes us unhappy which is why we move to new communities, change churches, drop out of social clubs only to join new ones which end up looking a lot like the ones we left. It is our unhappiness that causes us to assume others must live equally less than joy-filled lives, but they are "dishonest" and only post highlights of the good times on social media. We do not trust those who might actually be happy and hence we "hate." It is our lack of knowing how to achieve happiness for ourselves that drives us to this abhorrence of others, to consume adult beverages at an alcoholic level, to gorge ourselves into obesity and poor health, and further escape reality with porn and gaming and politically heated debates and sport team obsession, just to name a few.

The list of ways we mask our unhappiness is much more extensive than what I have written but, in the end, we find ways not to answer the question. But we want to, we need to, and we can. It is possible to create a definition that we can not only attain, but sustain.

One reason it is possible to define happiness such that it is attainable and, more importantly, sustainable, is because we can redefine the foundation upon which we build our happiness. For example, we equate happiness with that which comes for a source of which we do not know. Remember, the definition is based on "luck." With such a definition, of course we are frustrated. If you cannot know the source, you cannot do anything to get more of that which comes from this source. In the end, it is as if we live in a cruel game of the gods as believed by the Romans and Greeks with their mythology of deities who behaved more like impetuous and fickle humans than benevolent and gracious entities.

But happiness is not from a source that is not knowable or, worse, volatile. Happiness is attainable because it comes from a Source that has given us a formula, a way to gain and sustain love, joy, peace, and freedom in every area of life. Once we apply this formula to one area of our life and experience its results, we can turn to any area and watch our lives improve not just qualitatively but quantitatively.

Let's be clear: I am a very "material" girl. I operate in a physical world, amongst tangible objects, and I believe in what I can see and manipulate with my tactile senses. I am a physical being after all. It is important to know that happiness is not something that can become your reality because you "think" it or "feel" it or "believe" it. Happiness is tangible!

And please let's not play that "I am full of joy" game where we define happiness as related to circumstances and joy is what transcends the moment. Whatever. We all know we want to be happy and we all know it is both a "feeling" and a "thing" and, as such, let's accept that happiness is real and possible and it is both ethereal and factual. Intangible and tangible. Spiritual and Real.

If happiness did not have a tangible, quantifiable reality, I, me, and myself, as an academic, as a social scientist schooled in the scientific methodology, an analytic, a skeptic, someone who needs to see proof documented over multiple applications and in myriad settings, I would not trust, believe, accept it. As such, this is not a book about how to "think" your way into happiness. This is a book about how to "act" your way into happiness. It is a formula, after all. It is math, and numbers do not lie.

Happiness is an efficient process. It is a simple equation. No one ever said anything that is good and even great is easy, but so much of what is great is simple. To have the highest HQ (Happiness Quotient) possible, one must be able to say something along the lines of:

IQ – I am a lifelong learner always seeking new insights and new knowledge, and I am open to input which may cause me to exclaim, "Well, holy smokes, I was wrong this whole time. I need to adjust my thinking and therefore what I am doing." It is exciting to learn although it can be a challenge at times because so much of what I know is not part of what is deemed "common knowledge" and certainly not easily accessible via a five-minute internet search.

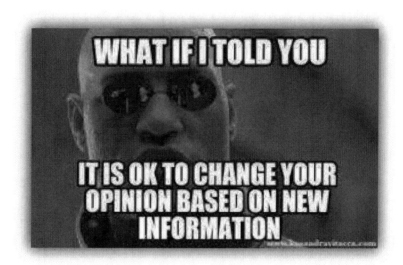

EQ – My actions match the data, stats, facts, patterns, and information I have received and I don't delude myself in any way. I do not rationalize and justify why I am experiencing the results of all I sow. Rather, I own my awesomeness as well as my deficiencies. Even when I don't like the options I can ascertain in the present moment, I know I always have a choice. I have never been and will never be a victim. I am fully capable of having it "all" because I define "all."

GQ – There is a God of the Universe, and I am not it. I did not create the world nor myself, and I know this God has only the best, the most, the greatest in His eternal plans for me so I need not fret or worry no matter how "bad" I have been or even might be in the future. Even in the midst of what I deem "evil," my God has it all under control and loves me more than I love myself so Life, in the here and now and beyond, will be better than good, it will be great!

If you can articulate something to that effect about your Intellectual Quotient, Emotional Quotient, and your God Quotient, then the only outcome should be the ability to sustain the highest Happiness Quotient.

But what if this is not your experience? What if that is precisely why you are reading this book – something is off. Maybe you were happy once and just can't get back there. Or, maybe you have never felt truly, sustainably happy in all areas of your life and you want to.

"The Happiness Formula" works. It is real. It is tangible. It is quantifiable and qualifiable, and it will take time. I always hesitate to tell people that I discovered "The Happiness Formula" after a decade in hell. But, anything that is worth having, is worth fighting for and it is my hope you will fight for your happiness.

Before we can get there, however, we have to confront two major barriers: (1) the list we all carry in our heads; the list which defines what will make us happy, – our litmus test, and (2) our sense of entitlement, our expectations, and our inability to recognize the world was not created for our personal pleasure.

BARRIER 1: THE LITMUS TEST

In science, a "litmus test" is a test to establish the acidity or alkalinity of a mixture. In life, to apply a litmus test is to identify what the critical element is that will indicate future success or failure. A Litmus Test is what we expect of ourselves and others. It is the standard by which we measure ourselves and others. Whether one is cognizant of or is even willing to admit they have such a test, identifying this list you have set for yourself is essential to achieve happiness.

Knowing what it is that we identify as "success" for ourselves, what will bring us "happiness" is quite often a list that is not factual. We have these ideas that we hold in our head and around which we structure our lives and make decisions. When we begin to use our intellect (IQ) and examine them against the data, facts, and stats, the research, we will discover we might be wrong. Or, when we begin to examine the standards we have set against our emotional selves (EQ), we might realize we don't even want what we have been striving for all along.

In order to understand "The Happiness Formula" as a formula that can be applied to any area of life such that you get what you really want, we have to eventually accept that we have a checklist, a standard, a litmus test which we MUST examine so we can determine if it has criteria we want to keep or discard.

So what does a typical litmus test look like? For a large percentage of people, it involves a certain level of monetary attainment. Along the same lines, people have a title, a career position in mind which for them, indicates they have "made it." For those who measure themselves based on the achievement of their children, you won't be truly happy until your child gets accepted to college, a top 10 university ups the ante, and a full-ride puts you over the top of your standard of success and happiness. We tend to get pulled into the comparison game, "Where do you live?" "What kind of car do you drive?" "Where did you go on your last family vacation?" These help us assess how well we have done in life and how we rank compared to others. We are not sure what makes us happy, so we let the ranking tell us.

You will know someone has a litmus test by the following statements:

- By the time I am 30, I want to be married and have a home because I want to be done with making babies by 35.
- When these kids leave the house, I will be so happy. Being a parent is exhausting!
- When I get to be CEO of my company, I will have hit the big time, baby!
- When I get to finally leave this corporate crap and be a full-time entrepreneur, life will be sweet!
- I want to be a millionaire by the time I am 50.
- When I lose all this extra weight, I will be unstoppable.
- By the time I am 60, I will retire with enough money to maintain the lifestyle to which I have become accustomed.

- When I get married, life will be so much easier because this single life is hard and lonely.
- When I get divorced, life will be so much better because this married life is hard and lonely.

By the time... When... Then... One day I will be happier. While a rational adult would be hard pressed to admit they are disenchanted with their present reality, this language is a daily occurrence and it reveals a lack of sustainable happiness. It is so pervasive, so subtle that the idea that one can be happy at this moment, at present, regardless of the circumstances is usually a belief reserved for those more "spiritual." It's as if to be happy, we must compare ourselves to outcomes we can quantify and qualify. Synonyms for happiness are "favorable, propitious, successful, and prosperous." Because our society, our parents, have established a list of what happiness means and what it looks like, we seldom examine if this list has anything to do with what accentuates our unique gifts and desires.

As the president of my high school class, I fulfilled the customary role of hosting the ten-year reunion. I had moved out of state, but many of my fellow graduates were still in California, so we had a good turnout. One woman who I had known casually since elementary school approached me to chat.

"It's good to see you, Kasandra. I assume your life is going well?" There was something in her body language and tone of voice that led me to believe she was either nervous, in a hurry, or not at ease. I tried to sound calm and jovial because, alas, I was pretty sure this was the first time she and I had ever spoken. "Life is really good. As you can tell I will have a baby in about another month. How have you been these past ten years?" She blurted, "I am just as successful as you. I know you were voted 'Most Likely to Succeed,' but I could have easily won that award too. I just wanted you to know I have done very well." And she walked away. To this day, I have never heard from her again.

A male friend of mine relayed the story of calling his ex-wife to boast about his promotion and pay raise. They have been divorced for over 20 years and he has remarried. Yet, the first person he calls is someone who he admits he wanted to "shove it in her face." He told me it was probably immature of him to drive his new $80,000 Mercedes in front of her house, but she always put him down when they were married. She constantly reminded him how poorly he did as a provider for her and the children. Thus, to finally have arrived at a monetary level and job status which would allow him to provide more than enough, gave him great satisfaction. He had made it. HIs standard was that of his ex-wife and, in his mind, he finally measured up.

When my friend relayed this story, my first response was to be embarrassed for his immaturity in the face of an achievement. But as he continued speaking, I sensed his pain. I felt his years of hurt and I began to pray that this would be the beginning of his unbinding. He had spent years bound up in the pain of a standard that may or may not have been his (i.e., earning $X annually). This standard may have originated in his formative years in school. It reminded me of what happened at my 10-year reunion. My two friends felt the need to confront their "demon," which they had made another person. It is easier to do this than to confront the real perpetrator of the unhappiness, themselves.

For some of us, there may not be a specific person with whom we measure ourselves, but rather an image we are trying desperately to uphold.

I had not spoken to Henry in over a decade, so when he called me out of the blue, I was curious. He informed me he had been following me on Facebook and noticed I traveled on a lot of Carnival cruises and wanted to know if had I traveled with other cruise lines and how they compared. While I was familiar with two other brands, I mostly traveled with Carnival simply because each time I had specific dates in mind, they had been the most convenient choice. I was not opposed to other cruise lines; Carnival was just the company that made the most sense for what I was doing at the time.

Then he confessed his real question, "What about the people? I heard they are pretty low class." I addressed his question with honesty insofar as my experience. I have found that whether I am drinking $20 shots at the Ritz in business suits and high heels or swigging a beer with the local bikers at the river, everyone is getting drunk and acting the fool. Therefore, I choose not to drink. Wherever I go, the sober, mature adults behave about as "high class" as I "require."

We have a litmus test, conscious or not, to determine if we are tracking towards a standard. Because of how I grew up, to earn $100,000 a year was an indicator I had made it but for my ex-husband who grew up with parents who were worth about $85 million when we met, he had to earn $500,000/year or, in his mind, he was nothing.

Our litmus test is tied to the standards set by those closest to us.

We start this process in our childhood innocently enough. When I was in elementary school in the 70s, we frequently played a game designed to tell our future. (see image) Each of the four choices had to contain a choice you would not want for your future. For example, M stood for Mansion, A = Apartment, S = Shack, and H = House. When you examine this childhood game, we were reinforcing what society defines as some of the criteria in a litmus test: (1) The type of house you own is important, and everyone wanted the mansion. (2) It matters who you marry because of course you will get married. (3) Having children is part of what society values and therefore you will have them. And (4) The kind of car you drive is one of the first ways you can declare you have "made it."

	M	A	S	H	
Mercedes					Good Looking Boy
Rolls Royce					Gonna be CEO Boy
Bentley					Future Sport Pro Boy
Chevette					Awkward Nerdy Boy
	1	2	3	10	

Some might object, "Come on, Kasandra. It's a childhood game. It's innocent." I humbly submit, if you are not intentional about what you allow and disallow, your children are absorbing values which define their thoughts, their actions, their character, and their future. If we are not vigilant to help them understand the power of the myriad influences around them that tell them what to believe and what to value, their

Litmus test will look at lot like the list that creates a high level of unhappiness when people hit mid-life starting in the 40s.

When you consider that men take their life almost four times as much as women and account for seven out of every 10 suicides, a rate that is highest in middle age,[1] slowing down long enough to examine what you have absorbed as "truths" and what might really be "lies" is critical if one is to have a shot at being happy. Thus, being intentional early in the life of someone is one way to raise enough awareness so that, ideally, this person will start the process of authentic self-identification and self-definitions which allow for healthy boundaries and effective life choices.

Be aware that a litmus test is being written for you, telling you who you should be, what you should want, how you should look, who you should marry, etc. If you don't realize the litmus test is being written for you, you may live in a rebellious assertion of self, demanding others like you just the way you are. Or you could experience the opposite, which is constant defeat and disappointment – because you can never measure up. Ultimately, you will participate in choosing a side, separating yourself from others, so that you can take comfort in having identified the "enemy." You will project your fears onto others.

Fear very often causes some of us to look outside of our ugliness and deflect. Casting judgment on someone is easier than deciphering why the life of that person bothers me so

---

[1] https://afsp.org/about-suicide/suicide-statistics/ Men die by suicide 3.53x more often than women. White males accounted for 7 of 10 suicides in 2016. The rate of suicide is highest in middle age — white men in particular.

darn much. Someone's lifestyle, their marriage, their accomplishments, the way they speak, dress, act, etc., very often causes jealousy or envy in the weak but, equally and quite possibly more than is made public, inspiration and empowerment for the strong.

In recovery programs for those with addictive behaviors, they use the expression "Egomaniac with an inferiority complex" to describe this phenomenon. You are either so much "better than" you cannot get along and get what you want from life and others. Or, you are so much "worse than" you cannot get along and get what you want from life and others! While some people are inclined to extremes and therefore have to spend a lot more time finding the criteria that will allow them to be comfortable in their skin, every person has some semblance of a skewed Litmus Test, which must be examined over time. When you consider a common response to, "How's work?" is, "Work would be great if it weren't for the people," It is clear that it is our inability to deal with life and people that must be addressed not, necessarily, a wholesale change of life and the people in it.

After all, an attitude that causes one to have to defend who they are at the slightest hint of another's questioning is NOT freedom or expression of one's individuality. A leader, a person at peace with self, a person who knows who they are and to whom they belong does not need to prove themselves to others any more than the lion needs to prove himself to the sheep.

At this point, you might be thinking, "Well are you supposed to 'want' anything?! And what about goals? Can we have goals for our future without them being defined by someone else? How are we supposed to train a young person to go for their dreams? Is it wrong to set our sights on achieving straight 'A's, winning the spelling bee, becoming the starting quarterback, or first chair in the orchestra? Or, in the case of a person in middle-age, is it wrong to want to become the person in charge or achieve a certain level of monetary wealth or have a sexy, six-pack ab body?"

Having goals is critical to success. Research proves this. Those who define goals, write their goals, review their goals, and ask someone to hold them accountable to them, achieve their goals. Not only that, they make more money! Goal setting and annual planning is required to achieve life goals, so they are part of "The Happiness Formula." We need to "shoot for the stars" and create "vision boards" and "hang out with the winners." Motivational speakers assure us, "You are the five people you hang out with most." Goals and aspirations are good. Until they are not.

There is nothing inherently "wrong" or "bad" with a litmus test. Having a standard against which to measure yourself is vital to success and happiness. But unfortunately, often the ends justify the means. At some point, an adult will look back and, in pursuit of a specific outcome, they will realize they never took enough time to determine WHY this specific outcome is the standard they set for themselves in the first place. Or, they will look up one day in their 40s and realize, I am not where I said I would be, where I want to be, where I had hoped to be – and I have NO idea what to do now.

A classic example is almost every family in the United States is convinced a four-year college degree is the pinnacle of success for their child. We assume that it is the degree which will "guarantee" their child's access to higher level titles/positions and, hence, more money. The underlying belief and assumptions are numerous, and research may not always prove the actual outcome is worth it. Yet, almost 70% of high school graduates will start the college journey[1] costing themselves and/or their family money and time that does not always translate into better jobs, more money and certainly not happiness. The standard of college as the litmus test for success and happiness is pervasive. Some adults have successful careers without going to college and yet many will spend thousands of dollars and hundreds of hours getting a college degree because they believe they have not "made it" without the piece of paper confirming and validating their success.

Even if you cannot relate to or cannot accept that pursuing college may not be as "fool-proof" as you had hoped, consider the standards we set for our bodies. No matter how many body-positive magazines hit the racks, no matter how many memes get shared which applaud even the most rotund physique, the standard of excellence is healthy and svelte without rolls or bulges. To be healthy, it is known, one must eat clean, exercise regularly, drink water over alcohol, sleep at least eight hours per night, meditate, pray. Yet we adamantly defend our "right" to live any way we please (drink and eat in a gluttonuos fashion such that our bodies reflect our

---

[1] Of the 3.1 million people ages 16 to 24 who graduated from high school between January and October 2016, about 2.2 million, or 69.7 percent, were enrolled in college in October 2016. https://www.bls.gov/opub/ted/2017/69-point-7-percent-of-2016-high-school-graduates-enrolled-in-college-in-october-2016.htm

negligence) and then feel offended when we are not considered "sexy."

So if someone were to ask me, "How do I look?" and what she was wearing was not flattering, I would say, "Your beauty does not shine through in that outfit." But if I am pressed further and asked, "Do I look fat?" I don't want to be manipulated into not telling the truth so I will respond, "You are overweight." At this point, however, I risk being labeled "mean" or "cruel" and yet you know the standard as well as I. Let's not undermine our happiness by wishing the facts were not true. Don't insist that you loved ones participate in your self-delusion.

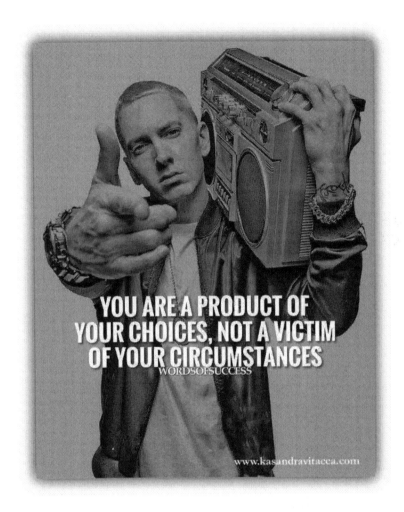

On college campuses, there is a notion called "vindictive protectiveness." This is the practice of giving more weight to feelings over facts. This trend is worth examining. The problem with this approach is our Litmus Test is warped because feelings are not facts. Feelings change. And, as such, we are setting up our young people for failure.

The ultimate aim, it seems, is to turn campuses into "safe spaces" where young adults are shielded from words and ideas that make some uncomfortable. And more than the last, this movement seeks to punish anyone who interferes with that aim, even accidentally. You might call this impulse *vindictive protectiveness*. It is creating a culture in which everyone must think twice before speaking up, lest they face charges of insensitivity, aggression, or worse.

But vindictive protectiveness teaches students to think in a very different way. It prepares them poorly for professional life, which often demands intellectual engagement with people and ideas one might find uncongenial or wrong. The harm may be more immediate, too. A campus culture devoted to policing speech and punishing speakers is likely to engender patterns of thought that are surprisingly similar to those long identified by cognitive behavioral therapists as causes of depression and anxiety. The new protectiveness may be teaching students to think pathologically.

Because there is a broad ban in academic circles on "blaming the victim," it is generally considered unacceptable to question the reasonableness (let alone the sincerity) of someone's emotional state, particularly if those emotions are linked to one's group identity. The thin argument "I'm offended" becomes an unbeatable trump card. This leads to what Jonathan Rauch, a contributing editor at this magazine, calls the "offendedness sweepstakes," in which opposing parties use claims of offense as cudgels. In the process, the bar for what we consider unacceptable speech is lowered further and further.

Out of fear of federal investigations, universities are now applying that standard—defining unwelcome speech as harassment—not just to sex, but to race, religion, and veteran status as well. Everyone is supposed to rely upon his or her own subjective feelings to decide whether a comment by a professor or a fellow student is unwelcome, and therefore grounds for a harassment claim. Emotional reasoning is now accepted as evidence.

If our universities are teaching students that their emotions can be used effectively as weapons—or at least as evidence in administrative proceedings—then they are teaching students to nurture a kind of hypersensitivity that will lead them into countless drawn-out conflicts in college and beyond. Schools may be training students in thinking styles that will damage their careers and friendships, along with their mental health.[1]

Just because you have not reached your goal doesn't mean you won't ever reach it. But be sure it is the right goal for you. Focus on what is real and true, the data, facts and stats. Then apply your IQ to the process of gathering this information. Next, analyze all that information through your EQ to figure out who you really are and who you really want to be. Decide

---

[1] https://www.theatlantic.com/magazine/archive/2015/09/the-coddling-of-the-american-mind/399356/

your truth for today. Tomorrow you can make a different decision.

In the end, the Litmus Test is real. It is created for us when we are young, and we either accept it and seek to please those who created it for us whether those from whom we seek approval is a parent or some other authority figure or society at large. Or we rebel against the standards and convince ourselves we are unique individuals who will pave our happy destiny only to eventually discover all we have done in life is make choices opposite of the standard others set for us. By mid-life many will be in crisis not knowing whether they agree with any of their life choices, hence, the "mid-life crisis."

Here are two choices: (1) you can either go the way of death via self-forgetting – alcohol, pills, gaming, porn, affairs, sexual conquest, food, sports fanaticism, heated political activism, blaming, isolation, even suicide, or (2) you can seek life which requires the shedding of the self and world-imposed definitions to walk into the unknown, to seek new possibilities, and break out of the cocoon to fly free, transformed.

BARRIER 2: EXPECTATIONS

The final elephant in the room we must examine before we dive into the specifics of "The Happiness Formula" and explore examples of how to apply it to various areas of our life: our expectations for what life "should" deliver to us because we "deserve" it. This attitude is grounded in a belief that the world has been created for our pleasure. But what about everyone else? At what point does my pursuit of my needs and desires trample on your pursuit of your needs and desires? At what point do I surrender my needs and desires so you can pursue yours? Is there an option in which we all get "enough" – and what exactly is "enough"?

Or, is it possible that we can all have as much as we need and desire without limits? Is it possible that each of us can live unhindered in the process of getting what we need and want? Can we somehow arrange for everyone to live just like they want without any interference or judgment?

Is this the real goal? Is that what we assume will give us "happiness"?

For far too many, the answer is "yes." We want to live with impunity while requiring everyone else to follow rules, so we can live with impunity! Unfortunately, we have to consider others in everything we do. The boundary between my individuality and your individuality is more like a dotted line than a solid line. It is a fence low enough to sit on, see to the other side, and even step over. It is not a solid, high wall which cannot be scaled. We do not live on an island. Everything we do and say has an impact on others. We are our "brother's keeper," but we are not each other's Source.

The world was not created for my pursuit of pleasure. The world was designed for us to live in community, within families, as couples, all of which honor the role of the individual to participate in his or her unique way to bring Light, Life, and Unity to the whole. As such, to ignore the need for that which so many want to argue is "relative" – i.e., morality – is to ignore the very fabric of who we are as unique creations made in the image of a magnificent, holy, and perfect God.

To pursue a "moral life" requires each of us to tap into the Supernatural within and around each of us (GQ) if we are to have any chance of engaging our IQ to glean insight, understanding, and wisdom such that we engage our EQ which allows us to transform ourselves into vessels of purpose and value, impact and influence.

And this is precisely what Lord Rabbi Sachs wants us to understand when he held a series of radio broadcasts "Morality in the 21st Century" with leading philosophers, thinkers, innovators and philanthropists, as well as students from across the country. "The thesis I wanted to test was that for the past 50 years the West has been engaged in a fateful experiment: that we can do without a shared moral code. Words that once guided us — like "right", "wrong", "ought", "should", "duty", "obligation", "loyalty", "virtue", "honor" — now have an antiquated air about them, as if they come from an age long dead."[1]

Rabbi Sachs says the solution to the global moral crisis lies in the message of the High Holy Days, "On Rosh Hashanah, Yom Kippur and the days between, we enact one of Judaism's most powerful yet unfashionable beliefs: that *our lives individually and collectively have a moral dimension*."[2] [emphasis mine.] This is the "GQ" of "The Happiness Formula."

To acquire and sustain a high quotient of happiness (HQ) one must maintain a constant dance with Individual Acquisition of Knowledge/Information (IQ) + Awareness of the Collective in which the IQ and Who we are as sentient beings is applied (EQ) + Morality That Transcends All of It and Allows for "Perfection" amidst all the messiness (GQ).

While it is worth listening to the podcast series hosted by Lord Rabbi Sachs, "Morality in the 21st Century," a few excerpts from "The Jewish Chronicle" article highlight the interplay between self, community, and God:

> "We've outsourced morality to the market and the state. The market gives us choices; the state deals with the consequences, but neither passes any kind of judgment on those choices. So long as we don't directly harm anyone else, we are free to do whatever we like."

---

[1] "Why the World Needs Rosh Hashanah" The Jewish Chronicle, September 7, 2018. https://www.thejc.com/comment/comment/why-the-world-needs-rosh-hashanah-jonathan-lord-sacks-1.469442

[2] Ibid.

"This was experienced at the time as a huge liberation. We were freer to be whatever we choose to be than humans have ever been before. But we can now count the costs in broken families, loss of community, a rise in depression, teenage suicides and loneliness, a loss of trust in big corporations and governments, the new tribalism of identity politics, and the vitriol that passes for communication on the internet. A shared morality binds us together. Lose it, and people find themselves vulnerable and alone."

"We move from a world of "We" to one of "I": the private pursuit of personal desire."

"The bottom line of all of this is that society needs more than the free market and the liberal democratic state. It needs us to accept moral responsibility for our own lives and the common good. That truth has been in eclipse for half a century, but the strains are beginning to show. We have already seen the first tremors of the alternatives: populism, identity politics, the culture of victimhood, and the rise of the far left and far right — what I call the politics of anger."

"Long ago Jews pioneered the alternative: the politics of hope. Hope is born when we dedicate ourselves individually and collectively to justice, compassion, the sanctity of life and the dignity of the individual. That is what we are summoned to do on Rosh Hashanah and Yom Kippur. God does not ask us to be perfect. He asks us to try our best to love Him, our neighbor and the stranger. And when we fail, as we all do one way or another, He asks us to acknowledge our failures and try again."

So, now that we have identified the elephant, how do we eat it? You guessed it, one bite at a time.

We will examine each aspect of "The Happiness Formula" both at a high level as well as ways we can incorporate it into our life practically, so we increase our Love, Joy, Peace, Freedom – HAPPINESS!

IQ – INTELLECTUAL QUOTIENT

Information, Data, Facts, Stats, Patterns, Research – The Technical side of Knowing

An intelligence quotient (IQ) is a total score derived from several standardized tests designed to assess human intelligence. Approximately two-thirds of the population scores are between IQ 85 and IQ 115. About 2.5 percent of the population scores above 130, and 2.5 percent below 70.

> *"The test confirms she is a genius, Ms. Vitacca. We'd like to send her to a special school for "Mentally Gifted Minds" where she will be more challenged and surrounded by children like her."*

> *"That is great, but I am a single, working mother. I can't afford to send her to a special school and how will I get her there because I work far away and…"*

> *"Ms. Vitacca, you don't have to worry about anything. This is a special program that is paid for and we arrange for her transportation. We'd like to start her next year."*

When my mother told me I would attend a new school for fifth and sixth grade, my only thought was, "What about my friends?" She made me promise that no matter how badly I wanted to come home, I would commit to a year at the MGM program and if at the end of my fifth-grade year I still wanted to return to my former elementary, she would let me finish six grade with the kids with whom I had grown up.

By Christmas break, I was in tears. I loved learning, and I enjoyed the challenge and rigor of the classes, but the kids were all from "normal" families. One little girl was mean and judgmental. She was a "good Christian" girl from an upper-middle-class family with a mother and father who took the children on annual family vacations to Hawaii and church every Sunday. I felt like Jo to her Blair[1], and I wanted to go back to the friends I knew.

While I was aware at a young age that I wanted more out of life than living paycheck to paycheck with the biggest excitement centered around a weekend of partying at the local river, I did not feel like I fit in at this new school. However, my mother made me promise I would stay the course because she knew education was the key to making it in life and if I had been given the gift of a high IQ, then I had better use it to my advantage.

So I accepted the idea that to "get ahead," to better myself, I would have to leave my old friends, my old ways, my old self, behind.

---

[1] "The Facts of Life" was a popular TV show when I grew up. It was an American sitcom that originally aired on NBC from August 24, 1979, to May 7, 1988, making it one of the longest-running sitcoms of the 1980s. The series focuses on Edna Garrett (Charlotte Rae) as she becomes a housemother at the fictional Eastland School, an all-female boarding school in Peekskill, New York. Blair's chief foil was Jo. The two made no secret of their mutual dislike: Jo found Blair spoiled and snobbish; Blair thought Jo was rude and crude. However, more than once Blair stuck up for and stood by Jo in her time of need (and vice versa), and eventually the two developed a much friendlier relationship. In one episode, Jo even declared Blair as her official best friend.

By the time I entered high school, I was driven in a way that intimidates people. The phrase "good is the enemy of great" had not been popularized by Jim Collins yet, but I already knew and embraced it. So much so that my addictive tendencies began to manifest in high school, but it would take almost 20 more years for me to fully understand that our God-given instincts can far exceed their intended purpose. Until such time that I had to confront my addictive personality, however, I assumed my success was largely a product of my intellect.

After all, this is the story we tell ourselves about what is important, isn't it? Listen to any parent, and even if they don't say it directly, they constantly measure their child against others. They may play Beethoven and Bach while in the womb ("because it has been proven to increase IQ"). They may limit tv-watching time to only a few hours on the weekend. They may remove all high fructose corn syrup from their children's diet. Parents are obsessed with ensuring their child has a leg up when it comes to education, because education is considered the key to success.

As a financial advisor for over a decade, I realized that to show a parent the economic ignorance of saving no money for their retirement but spending upwards of $100,000 to ensure their precious little one does not have any concerns or struggles while in college, was akin to trying to convince an atheist to accept God. Our culture has so idealized children (or is it that we have heightened the subtle insidiousness of guilt?) that all logic and intellect has gone by the wayside.

Is education important? It is vital! It is critical. It is the foundation of "The Happiness Formula" – but at what cost?

Are you giving up "great" to get what is easier and faster and even "good"? Are you doing what the masses do for fear of being left behind or have you thought through what it all means? Have you spent enough time understanding all that is possible or, again, are you just doing what everyone says is the "right" thing to do?

While I assert that to pay for a child's education when you as a parent have not established all you need to guarantee your future is illogical, there are myriad examples of people doing that which is NOT logical. People make choices all the time based on how they "feel" rather than facts, data, stats, patterns, research, and logic. Our brains are wired for such decision making.

When you see something, hear something, feel something, smell something, the brain first processes that information as an emotion. The emotion is the oldest part of the brain, the most developed, and the most "basic." Its sole job is to answer the question, "Will I be eaten or can I eat this?" It is the "fight or flight" part of our brain. The amygdala sits at the base of our head closest to our spine. Input enters our brain and is processed through what has kept humans and animals alive for eons.[1] However, our brains also have a pre-frontal cortex which houses the newest and final part of our brain to develop. That part of the brain allows us, as opposed to animals, to use logic, analyze data, create order, and employ rational thought.[2] It is Dr. Spock to the amygdala's Mr. Hyde.

---

1 "The Amygdala's Location and Function in the Brain," September 3, 2018, Regina Bailey, ThoughtCo.
https://www.thoughtco.com/amygdala-anatomy-373211
2 https://www.goodtherapy.org/blog/psychpedia/prefrontal-cortex

A visual is that of the elephant and the rider. The elephant represents the part of our brain that houses our feelings, our emotions, and our "fight or flight" reactionary nature. The rider represents the part of our brain which houses our logical, rational, reasoning nature that organizes information. It arrives at a solution based on information it has previously been given. The rider sits on top of the elephant holding onto reigns believing he controls the elephant simply by pulling to the right or the left or kicking his heels into the elephant's hide or shouting commands.

Despite the rider's best attempts, if the elephant senses a threat or wants to go another direction, the rider is just along for the ride.

In our hubris, we want to believe we approach life and all decisions with logic and reason. We convince ourselves that our financial decisions make sense and will secure us the future we desire. We tell ourselves that our diet and exercise practices are good enough to live well into our later years and ensure a high quality of life. We defend our decisions on most anything with vigor and adamancy that borders on anger in the face of a factoid, data point, and research which might prove us wrong.

In recovery programs for addictive behaviors, professionals and lay practitioners seek to help others by "sponsoring" them through a 12-step process. One step is to take a "personal inventory" of all the wrongs and abuse suffered at the hands of another. The goal is to list every person, institution, and ideology we believe harmed us, to identify anyone or anything which has kept us from living the life we desire.

The next step is to discuss this inventory with a "sponsor" who will allow the "sponsee" to explain this harm emotionally. Eventually, the sponsor asks, "What role did you have in this?"

The goal of inventory work is the IQ and EQ of "The Happiness Formula" insofar as you use your IQ to identify facts, data, and stats while moving into EQ – what is real? What role did you play in it? One is to engage her IQ to review the past and clearly articulate the facts, data, and patterns to determine what is real without judgment, to define what was and even a bit of what is. Then, by reviewing the past, patterns will emerge which will lead one to realize – I may not have all the facts or may even be wrong. For example, you assume someone stole your boyfriend because it hurts too much to consider he simply was not that into you. Or, you assume someone is cold-hearted because you can't fathom why someone would not want to be a "hugger." While we may not always like all the data and facts we discover, they are just that, data and facts, with no emotion attached.

In Step Four of the recovery process, as defined by the book "The 12x12," we acknowledge we have God-given "instincts" that serve a purpose. Unfortunately, far too often these instincts far exceed their intended purpose. Some of them no longer serve us well. "Nearly every serious emotional problem can be seen as a case of misdirected instinct. When that happens, our great natural assets, the instincts, have turned into physical and mental liabilities."[1] The book goes on to explain that the cause of our unhappiness is this battleground of instincts:

---

[1] "Twelve Steps and Twelve Traditions," Alcoholic Anonymous World Services, Inc. 1952. Fortieth printing, 2004. p.42

65

Every time a person imposes his instincts unreasonably upon others, unhappiness follows. Demands made upon other people for too much attention, protection, and love can only invite domination or revulsion in the protector's themselves – two emotions quite as unhealthy as the demands which evoked them.[1]…When the satisfaction of our instincts for sex, security, and society becomes the sole object of our lives, then pride steps in to justify our excesses.

All the failings generate fear, a soul-sickness in its own right. Then fear, in turn, generates more character defects. Unreasonable fear that our instincts will not be satisfied drives us to covet the possession of others, to lust for sex and power, to become angry when our instinctive demands are threatened, to be envious when the ambitions of others seem to be realized while ours are not. We eat, drink and grab for more of everything that we need, fearing we shall never have enough. These fears are the termites that ceaselessly devour the foundations of whatever sort of life we try to build.[2]

In the 1992 movie loosely based on truth, "A Few Good Men," Jack Nicholson delivers what is one of the most memorable scenes in modern movie history as he shouts, "You can't handle the truth!" before his monologue of what is essentially data, facts, stats, patterns and, as such, truth. In the end, you may not always like what the facts reveal, you may not like your

---

[1] Ibid, p.44
[2] Ibid, p.49

choices as shown by the facts, but they are still factual, and you always have a choice.

Let's look at a financial example of what the uber majority believe is "right" but is not factual – buy term, invest the difference. We tell ourselves we will take the "savings" from the upfront cost of term insurance versus putting the money into a whole life insurance asset because we plan to put the differential in cost into an investment that will give us future growth.

Research proves over and over again people do not invest the difference.[1] They do not take the differential between what they are able to pay (save) and what they actually pay and put these "found" dollars in a place that will earn them something. Instead, they spend the money! This phenomenon is called Parkinson's Law, which is the adage that "work expands to fill the time available for its completion," put another way, "expenses rise to meet the level of income."

But even if you are the type of person who has overcome yourself such that you will take the "extra" money and apply it to an asset with growth for your future, there are other benefits, other facts which must be taken into consideration. In the case of term insurance, it is not an asset. It is necessary protection, but when you consider less than 2% of term insurance ever pays out (i.e.: the person does not die within the

---

[1] Bear in mind, if you are the type of person who has self-control and is actively saving your money somewhere, I encourage you to explore the foundational power of the world of investments combined with the world of non-direct recognition, dividend paying, whole life insurance from a mutual company. Visit www.financialepiphany.com to learn more.

term of the contract), the money you spent to protect your family is always lost.

If you had taken the time to fully understand the various assets available within the life insurance family of contracts and saved your money in the right whole life insurance asset, you would have not only actually incurred less cost, you would have a guaranteed, uninterrupted, compound interest, tax free asset that allows you to pay yourself a higher income in your "golden years" with the benefit that money will flow to your designated beneficiaries upon your demise. You would have spent less money and had a lot more but it takes time to learn, un-learn, and then implement that which is "great" versus what so many of us blindly and ignorantly accept as truth.

The point of examining this financial example is simply to highlight that IQ is about actually using it! If you apply "The Happiness Formula" to a very common "debate" (term v. whole life) the data, facts, and stats about the cost and "return" make the "right" choice clear…but that is not what happens. When you factor in the IQ and the EQ associated with learning about a much more complicated asset than most people will take the time to study, the answer is not so obvious. In the end, data, facts and stats must still be processed through one's personal belief system, one's lifestyle choices. Alone, IQ does not necessarily define the answer.

Ultimately, the real argument is not a variable of one factoid, a micro-economic analysis. It is about analyzing data to determine the best outcome. It is the macro analysis, the big picture long-term effects that might convince someone to change behaviors if they want different results.

For example, you saved a million dollars, and because you followed an "investment only" strategy with your money, at retirement you can withdraw a $35,000 annual income for the rest of your life. But if you spent more time learning how to allocate your investments and savings into a "personal pension" strategy, you could save the same $1 million and withdraw $75,000 to $90,000 annual income for the rest of your life.[1]

In the first scenario, you saved a million and had $35,000 annual income. In the second scenario, you have the same "net worth" because you saved a million and, yet, you get more than twice as much. I know which one I would choose.

1 "Optimizing Retirement Income by Combining Actuarial Science and Investments," Wade D. Pfau, Ph.D., CFA, 2015.
https://www.oneamerica.com/wps/wcm/connect/23b21fa6-8e9c-49c9-a49e-1a0b0ef95d91/OA_WP_Opt-Ret_Inc_05-15_web.pdf?MOD=AJPERES&CONVERT_TO=url&CACHEID=23b21fa6-8e9c-49c9-a49e-1a0b0ef95d91

Knowledge is power, but only if you know how to apply it and are willing to do the hard work to seek it. The power of IQ, regardless if you are barely educable or a genius, is you can ask questions. Research, ask, investigate, ask some more, question, research, ask, ask again. Your ability to think is your #1 tool to get financially stable, relationally secure, physically healthy – happy!

In the end, anything worth having is not easy to acquire. Period. So, if you ask, "Will it be easy?" the unequivocal answer is, "No!" But the more important question to ask is, "Will it be worth it?" because that answer is equally true and unconditional, "absolutely!"

In the United States of America we have an incredibly luxurious lifestyle, even the most disadvantaged among us. "The typical person in the bottom 5 percent of the American income distribution is still richer than 68 percent of the world's inhabitants."[1] Americans have a great lifestyle, but they do not have wealth. These are facts. One's IQ need not even be very high to understand the data...but are you willing to understand the implications?

Even as you move beyond the realm of money and examine the state of our physical health as a nation, the morale of our citizenry, the health of our overall communities, we have allowed ourselves to assume the acquisition of a degree is the stopping point of learning. Sure, we may give lip service to being a lifelong learner, but people are not learning. People do not read!

---

[1] "America's Poor Still Live Better Than Most Of The Rest Of Humanity. Tim Worstall, Forbes, June 1, 2013.

According to some studies, people who read at least seven business books a year <u>earn over 2.3 times more</u> than those who read only one book per year.[1] So why is reading considered boring? Why do people spend an average of five hours per night in front of the TV[2] and the average American does not read more than five books in a year?

Is it because despite having higher than average levels of educational attainment, adults in the United States have below-average basic literacy and numeracy skills (elementary grade level)[3] and books which contain the highest research and truth usually are written at a 9th to 10th grade level?[4] We have convinced ourselves that one must have a high IQ to "succeed" in life but IQ is not a number but a process, an attitude, a willingness to LEARN and never stop! Even if books might be "over your head," the only way to rise to the level of information that will transform your life is to invest the time to learn. Open the dictionary. Look up the hard words. Struggle a little. Reading burns more calories than watching TV[5] because when you engage with the written word, neurons fire which ignite your metabolism. TV is a pure escape and offers zero return.

---

[1] Sources: United States Department of Labor, Survey by Yahoo! Chief Solutions Officer Tim Sanders and Business Majors

[2] "How Much Do We Love TV? Let Us Count the Ways," John Koblin. New York Times, June 30, 2016

[3] "Troubling Stats on Adult Literacy," Megan Rogers. Inside Higher Ed. October 8, 2013

[4] "What Grade is Your Content Comprehension?" Alexander Macris. The Escapist. May 10, 2010

[5] "Did You Know: You Burn more Calories Sleeping than you do Watching Television?" www.news.dm February 06, 2013

Unfortunately, for far too many, they choose to ignore what is possible with the use of their IQ. Either they won't seek knowledge, or even in the face of it, they choose to ignore it. Thus, the popular "ignorance is bliss" philosophy becomes a mantra and the slow, steady, imperceptible slide into pain, confusion, disappointment, despair…and then rationalization and justification and blame begins. Alas, the slide begins because learning stops. Learning stopped because it is not "easy." It takes time. It causes you to question truths you thought you had already settled for yourself. Reading/Learning will cause you to look yourself in the mirror and honestly assess, "Am I happy?"

"The Happiness Formula" begins with IQ because it is the foundation of all Truth, all joy, peace, and freedom. You cannot become a better version of yourself, and you cannot reach the highest levels of happiness without the use of your intellect. We must learn and never stop!

In the end, the goal is to come to a place where you identify – everything in your past and present is just a data point, simply a factoid, an element of life on life's terms. Once we get clear on the data, facts, and patterns (IQ), we can transition into the EQ part of recovery.

You can be gut-level honest and expose yourself to the truth. Your past is not who you are, and the future is not here yet. Decide how you want to live today. The past hurts, habits, and hang-ups do not have to join you in your future. Do you want to take them with you? Do you want to remain in bondage to the pain and angst these past concerns create for you? Or would you rather leave them behind and get well?

One man was there who had been ill for thirty-eight years.

Yeshua, seeing this man and knowing that he had been there a long time, said to him, "Do you want to be healed?"

The sick man answered, "I have no one to put me in the pool when the water is disturbed; and while I'm trying to get there, someone goes in ahead of me."

Yeshua said to him, "Get up, pick up your mat and walk!"

Immediately the man was healed, and he picked up his mat and walked.[1]

I, like the man with the mat, had logical reasons why I was not well. My "superior" IQ helped me find many reasons why I was destined to be crippled. I had the consequences of my past bad choices that I had to carry with me. But eventually I was healed. Regardless of all his reasons, the man made a choice to trust the power of the God of the Universe to heal him, and so he walked.

---

[1] Complete Jewish Bible, John 5:5-9 www.biblegateway.com

EQ – EMOTIONAL QUOTIENT

Attitude, Awareness, Maturity, Self-Control

The capacity to be aware of, control, and express one's emotions, and to handle interpersonal relationships judiciously and empathetically. EQ is about relationships. How does what I am saying and doing affect YOU?

The car is moving so fast, and I can't seem to slow it down although I am in the driver's seat. With each new mountain curve, my fear and anxiety rise as not only do I barely miss going over the edge, I encounter drivers coming in the opposite direction, and I quickly swerve out of the way. At one point I simply lose control. The car speeds over the edge of the mountain and time slows to a snail's pace as everyone I know and love flashes through my mind because I will never see them again…

I am running as fast as I can, but my legs feel heavy, and I am out of breath. I know he has murdered others and now he is gaining on me. I cannot remember how I ended up alone in this dark, abandoned area of town but all I know is I have to get away. No matter how much I will myself to run faster, I seem to run even slower. I scream and cry hoping someone will hear me, but he grabs me…

It is a sunny school day and classes have been let out for lunch. I notice people looking at me with various expressions of awe, but I cannot determine if they are impressed with how I look or disgusted by me. I begin to feel self-conscious with the level of attention I am receiving so I slow down to look at my reflection in the windows of the school office. I am naked! What do I do now?!

During my elementary years, these nightmares were staples of my sleeping. I would always wake up just at the moment when the car was about to crash on the valley floor or the murderer had me in his grip or I realized I was walking around school naked. I had no idea how to save myself from death, devastation, and complete social ostracization. When I awoke, I was relieved to discover my fears were just nightmares, but I hated feeling powerless and vulnerable.

Specifically, I remember wondering, "How exactly did I end up in each of these situations in the first place? The moment was bad enough but what was worse was I realized it was choices I had made before the specific moment of horror that landed me in such a predicament? Somehow I knew I was not an innocent victim but, then again, how could I stop it all?

These recurring dreams stopped sometime during my teen years. I learned I could shape my reality by controlling my thoughts. I reasoned that if our conscious reality could be "altered," why not our subconscious, our dreams?

Before I went to bed, I told myself: You will not crash the car. You will confront and scare away the murderer, and you will always be clothed at school. Like Neo in the movie The Matrix,

I had taken the red pill.[1] When the Matrix was released in 1999, I immediately understood that many years earlier I too had decided to leave the perceived comfort of "ignorance" to pursue Truth. While Truth is a lot harder to grasp and more difficult to navigate, I also knew true sustainable happiness was possible.

To pursue truth at all costs will, indeed, cost you. But the rewards are far greater than what is possible to perceive at the moment. In order to achieve happiness we have to confront ourselves. The happiness journey has tangible, quantifiable rewards. The key is the elevation of the "Emotional Quotient."

Emotional intelligence is the key to both personal and professional success. Daniel Goleman is an author known around the world as an authority on "Emotional Intelligence."[2] Harvard Business Review's "10 Must Reads" for 2015 chose Goleman's work to open their book "On Emotional Intelligence." Goleman tells us,

---

[1] The term, popularized in science fiction culture, is derived from the 1999 film *The Matrix*. In the film, the main character Neo is offered the choice between a red pill and a blue pill by rebel leader Morpheus. The red pill represented an uncertain future—it would free him from the enslaving control of the machine-generated dream world and allow him to escape into the real world, but living the "truth of reality" is harsher and more difficult. On the other hand, the blue pill represented a beautiful prison—it would lead him back to ignorance, living in confined comfort without want or fear within simulated reality of the Matrix.
[2] Daniel Goleman is an internationally known psychologist who lectures frequently to professional groups, business audiences, and on college campuses. As a science journalist, Goleman reported on the brain and behavioral sciences for *The New York Times* for many years. His 1995 book, *Emotional Intelligence* was on *The New York Times* bestseller list for a year-and-a-half, with more than 5,000,000 copies in print worldwide in 40 languages, and has been a best seller in many countries.

"To be sure, intellect was a driver of outstanding performance. Cognitive skills such as big-picture thinking and long-term vision were particularly important. But when I calculated the ratio of technical skills, IQ, and emotional intelligence as ingredients of excellent performance, emotional intelligence proved to be twice as important as the others for jobs at all levels. Moreover, my analysis showed that emotional intelligence played an increasingly important role at the highest levels of the company, where differences in technical skills are of negligible importance."[1]

You can have all knowledge, but if you do not know how to apply that knowledge, you will not benefit from it. Here's why this is important. If you get what you want (a raise, a car, the spouse, etc.) you will likely not experience happiness if you EQ has not evolved.

I already had a high level of IQ that I worked hard to maintain with lifelong learning. But to be effective, I needed to learn to be empathetic, more mature, more self-controlled. I had my first "big" job as a young 30-something. I had a fancy title, a small staff, and a million-dollar budget. I answered to a board of directors, and my CEO hired an executive coach to work with me.

Ms. Dorothy was a classy woman in her 50s who had worked with executives her whole career. She had an impressive resume and home. I was eager to absorb all of her advice until she told me I needed to develop "humility." I argued with her,

---

[1] "HBR's 10 Must Reads On Emotional Intelligence," 2015. "What Make's a Leader" p.3

"People just need to do their job! I am not responsible for their feelings. They get paid to be excellent. If they want someone to stroke their ego, they need a friend or a dog, and I am neither."

My work life then was as tumultuous as my personal life. I could not keep a job longer than two years. By 2005, I was on job number too many to count and my second divorce. And I was not happy. I knew that I did not have a high enough EQ to be effective. So I called upon one of the only tools I knew well – my IQ – and I began to study, read, research, look for patterns, data, facts, and stats as they related to my life up to that point.

What was unequivocally clear was I did not make decisions with logic and rationale as my guide. I had lived much like most people. I made decisions with my emotions and justified my emotions with logic and facts.

I was being controlled by the oldest and most emotional part of my brain, the amygdala, which is much like that of the animals. I had to train myself to allow my emotions to travel to the frontal cortex, where my logic lives. I needed to learn to respond rather than react. The emotion center was telling me to trust no one. My logic center needed to analyze more closely.

Our brains need active intervention so we can respond logically and not emotionally. Angry outbursts harm our relationships and destroy our credibility.

> "Emotional Intelligence can reasonably be conceived as a measure of the degree to which a person

successfully (or unsuccessfully) applies sound judgment and reasoning to situations in the process of determining emotional or feeling responses to those situations. It would entail, then, the bringing of (cognitive) intelligence to bear upon emotions. It would encompass both positive and negative emotions. It would be a measure of the extent to which our effective responses were "rationally" based. A person with a high degree of emotional intelligence would be one who responded to situations with feeling states that "made good sense," given what was going on in those situations. Appropriately generated feeling states would serve as a motivation to pursue reasonable behavior or action. Emerging naturally out of "rational" emotions would be "rational" desires and "rational" behavior.[1]

Neurologically, synapses fire, electrical impulses are emitted which form grooves in our brain, and we need to physically change to force them out of the ruts they have created. Once these impulses are on fertile ground, it is possible to take in new information, form new attitudes and carry out new behaviors. Ultimately, what you feed your mind matters. There is no renewal, no transformation, without proper nourishment.

Increasing your EQ takes courage. As Winston Churchill so concisely put it, "Courage is what it takes to stand up and speak. Courage is also what it takes to sit down and listen." Unfortunately, as Churchill points out, "Men occasionally

---

[1] *Inquiry: Critical Thinking Across the Disciplines*, Winter, 1996. Vol. XVI, No. 2.
http://www.criticalthinking.org/pages/cognition-and-affect-critical-thinking-and-emotional-intelligence/485

stumble over the truth, but most of them pick themselves up and hurry off as if nothing ever happened."

Increasing one's emotional quotient is the dance between data, facts, stats, research and patterns and what this might mean for who you are, what you have done, where you might go, where you want to go, and do you even know what you want in the first place? If IQ is foundational to have a shot at happiness, EQ is the key that makes everything you know and understand come together to make sense for you. It is "the bringing of (cognitive) intelligence to bear upon emotions."

Tom Bilyeu is a filmmaker and serial entrepreneur who wants to solve what he calls a "pandemic" facing society – the poverty of poor mindset. In his empowerment blogs and videos, he emphasizes the ability one has to transform their life by changing how one thinks:

> It's hard to believe that the things we hold to be self-evident about the world and ourselves are, in fact, merely a construct—a series of conscious and unconscious decisions and beliefs that string together into a cohesive picture of how things are. This picture is, at least partially, a work of fiction. And that's a good thing because if it's a work of fiction, it can be rewritten to something more advantageous.
>
> That's the key insight that "The Matrix" gave me—not having the right skills is the only thing that's stopping me from being able to do kung fu, or fly a helicopter, or run my own company. Waking up to that idea caused me to begin asking a whole slew of new and

more empowering questions. I began to ask not what's possible, or what am I good at, but rather what do I want to accomplish and what do I need to learn to be successful at it? That to me is the key—to identify the gap in your skill set that stands between who you are today and who you need to be to accomplish your mission in life.

You don't have to want to save the world like Neo. But whatever it is, you can do it. This is only the Matrix after all.[1]

The only way to increase your EQ is to question your worldview and gauge your emotional temperature constantly. Then you can more clearly articulate the data, facts, and stats you believe to be true which shape your ideals and beliefs and how you act out that knowledge. As you get more honest about your feelings, you will increase your compassion for others, because you will see they are working on their feelings too.

A common statement one hears from corporate executives, retail cashiers, preachers, just about anyone who has worked long enough, "This job would be great if it weren't for the people." We all struggle with humanity. As such, how you respond to winning or losing, says a lot about how content and at peace you are with yourself. How happy are you purely because you exist as you?

My heart hurt for those who took to social media to express themselves about the last election. So many of the laments

---

[1] Tom Bilyeu www.impacttheory.com

included tears, rants and raves, and epithets directed at those who cast a vote other than their own. And, yet, these "adults" believed these public displays of emotion show they are "enlightened" or more "righteous." All those who complained and spewed negativity, from expressions of a loss of hope to those who felt the newly elected POTUS was akin to the appearance of the Second Coming, believed they were actually "correct" and "justified" in their opinions.

Negativity, judgmentalism, rationalization, and justification are emotionally draining. Those with low EQ are like the emperor with no clothes. They see themselves as the arbiters of critical thought and enlightenment, social justice, and whatever it is that makes them believe they are helping when they post their vitriol and foul language. However, what is happening is they are showing the world they will use the public airwaves as a platform for their less than joy-filled existence while they seek comrades to unite in mutual "hate."

If you suffer from belly fat, it is your stress-filled thinking, your focus on the negative, that keeps you pudgy.[1]

While that may seem like a non-sequitur and while this is not about negative-thought-created-belly-fat, it is about our ability to transform ourselves by taking our thoughts captive[2] so we can focus on all that is noble, pure, and admirable. In the process, you will be able to exercise out of yourself all that which is not noble, pure, and admirable within yourself (your "fat") so you experience greater joy regardless of your present circumstances![3]

---

[1] "Stress Raises Belly Fat, Heart Risks," Daniel J. DeNoon. www.webMD.com

[2] Do not conform to the pattern of this world, but be transformed by the renewing of your mind. Then you will be able to test and approve what God's will is—his good, pleasing and perfect will. (Romans 12:2 NIV)
So here's what I want you to do, God helping you: Take your everyday, ordinary life—your sleeping, eating, going-to-work, and walking-around life—and place it before God as an offering. Embracing what God does for you is the best thing you can do for him. Don't become so well-adjusted to your culture that you fit into it without even thinking. Instead, fix your attention on God. You'll be changed from the inside out. Readily recognize what he wants from you, and quickly respond to it. Unlike the culture around you, always dragging you down to its level of immaturity, God brings the best out of you, develops well-formed maturity in you. (Romans 12:1-2 The Message)

[3] 4 Rejoice in the Lord always. I will say it again: Rejoice! 5 Let your gentleness be evident to all. The Lord is near. 6 Do not be anxious about anything, but in every situation, by prayer and petition, with thanksgiving, present your requests to God. 7 And the peace of God, which transcends all understanding, will guard your hearts and your minds in Christ Jesus. 8 Finally, brothers and sisters, whatever is

Neuroscience abounds in research that proves we can rewire our brain. It is possible to alter our thought center, so we are in control of how we think, perceive ourselves, and experience life.[1]

Everyone is given the same number of hours in a day ("manna") and yet how is it that some experience joy and peace regardless of their circumstances and others only see misery and despair? How is it that some taste the sweet honey within their daily provision and have hope for many more days of joy, while others taste only the bitterness of this daily bread and cannot see beyond the brokenness of this temporal existence?

Sometimes our EQ is so underdeveloped that we cannot even see how we set ourselves up for failure. A somewhat innocuous email exchange provides an example of how subtle our ignorance is about the interplay of IQ and EQ. I belong to a group of "mature" women (generally 50 years and older). A woman asked the group what we thought of her tight outfit that revealed her mid-section. The majority of the responses were positive because of her fitness model physique. She was told to be confident and "flaunt it cuz you got it." But I was concerned that her clothes could reduce how much clients and coworkers respected her and felt comfortable around her.

It a fact of life that just because you can do something, does not mean you should. I used to dress provocatively too, but I learned that no matter how "liberated" you feel, society has an

true, whatever is noble, whatever is right, whatever is pure, whatever is lovely, whatever is admirable—if anything is excellent or praiseworthy—think about such things. (Philippians 4: 4-8 NIV)

[1] "How complaining physically rewires your brain to be anxious and depressed," www.theheartysoul.com. July 7, 2016

unconscious bias that tight, revealing clothes translate to loose morals. In the business world, that does not help achieve goals. I wore very little makeup and a professional hairstyle. But one day when I dressed in tight shorts and a crop top, a woman I met asked a colleague, "Is Kasandra a slut or something?"

This is still true today. When women act like teenagers at the office, posing with pouty lips and peace signs, colleagues and clients withdraw their respect. This is a fact of the working world. Our attire and our behavior need to affirm our expectation of respect. People have biases which you can disagree with and even label as close-minded and sexist. Their biases affect how they perceive you. You have to consider whether your desire to dress provocatively is improving your professional image or if it simply hampers your overall message. We train people how to treat us. What are we teaching them? This applies outside the office too. A husband worth having is looking for a woman with self-respect.

EQ also is about the capacity to control your emotions and be empathetic. When someone says or does something hurtful, remember that if they had known better, they would have done better. Ultimately, they are not doing it to you; they are just doing it. We can't honestly say "I don't care what people think." I care what people think. I consider them by the way I speak, act, and dress. I try to make choices that work for my goals while not letting other people's opinions define me. Embrace your uniqueness. When you truly love you, others will too.

Here is a joke that illustrates my point. Two friends, one an optimist and the other a pessimist, could never agree on anything. The optimist owned a hunting dog that could walk on water. He had a plan: Take the pessimist and the dog out duck hunting in a boat. They got out to the middle of the lake, and the optimist shot down a duck. The dog immediately walked out across the water, retrieved the duck, and walked back to the boat. The optimist looked at his friend and said, "What do you think about that?" The pessimist replied with a frown, "That dog can't swim, can he?"[1]

We view the world and life, others and ourselves through a lens that might be very different from others. While the joke applied labels of "good" and "bad" (i.e.: optimist and pessimist"), the "pessimist" uses a degree of logic to respond. As such, while the "optimist" may not like that his friend does not see the world as he does, his friend is not necessarily wrong or even "bad."

Give people enough room to be themselves considering you want the same for yourself. Remember, you can always choose another friend. The opinions, thoughts, beliefs of another do not need to distract from those which you hold for yourself.

---

[1] I want to thank the random person who posted this on Facebook. I wrote to you stating it would probably end up in my book and, voila. I hope its inclusion blesses you insofar as I am 99.9% certain you had no idea that your desire to provide a simple laugh would become a perfect illustration of EQ. Just because our world view, our perspectives, our style is not that of another, does not mean either of us is right or wrong, good or bad, better or worse. We are all just doing the best we can with what we know, who we are, and what we believe.

GQ – GOD QUOTIENT

Spiritual Connection to a Power Greater Than Yourself

> "I would hear people say 'God will solve all your problems' and I rebelled. 'Are you serious?! I tried that.' I tried to get good enough so God would give me what I want and it didn't work. What I figured out was, I wasn't praying to God. I was praying to Santa Claus."[1]

> "The fruit of the Spirit is love, joy, peace, patience, kindness, goodness, faithfulness, humility, self-control. Nothing in the Torah stands against such things." (Galatians 5:22-23)

A life that seeks God first is a life that is aware that IQ and EQ will only get you so far. Intelligence has a ceiling. Emotional energy has a limit. To live a life of abundance, joy, peace – happiness – one must submit both your finite IQ and EQ to that which has no end: a God of your understanding.

Educational entities tell us how to invest our mind to increase our IQ. Psychologists, behaviorists, counselors, neuroscientists, medical doctors, yogis, and anyone who can capture your attention will tell us how to invest our emotional energy to develop a more effective EQ. World religions and spiritual practices tell us how to invest our time so that we don't get caught up in the urgency of life that distracts us from

---

[1] An anonymous member in a 12-step recovery program sharing his path to find a god of his understanding.

focusing on what is ultimately most important – God as they understand it. (GQ)

Rabbi Lord Jonathan Sachs is a world-renowned voice for Judaism. He lays out ten "life-changing principles" as he helps his followers prepare for Rosh Hashanah and Yom Kippur.

In the intro to his blog, he states, "Judaism is the satellite navigation system of the soul, and Rosh Hashanah is the day we stop and see whether we need to change direction."[1] Whether your God is called Yeshua or Mohammed or Buddha, a person who does not commit themselves to a life ordered by a god they can name and a guidance system they can follow, (a spiritual discipline, a religious practice, a system to access God) will eventually veer off course.

In 2008, Arthur C. Brooks released a book, "Gross National Happiness," in which he researches to determine what makes people happy. For example, does having kids make you happier than those who don't have kids? Do the number of kids matter? Are liberal values more likely to bring happiness or conservative values? Does money make you happy or is it a matter of the amount of money? Does believing in God and following a religious/spiritual discipline make you happier than those who claim no system? We learn from the research that increased happiness is not whether you say you are affiliated with a particular spiritual practice, it is whether you practice that system.[2]

He goes on to add, "The correlation between religion and happiness has little to do with money, age, or education.

---

[1] http://rabbisacks.org/investing-time/ September 1, 2018
[2] Gross National Happiness, Arthur C. Brooks. 2008 Basic Books. P.43

Religious people are happier than secularists even if they are alike in these ways. If two people are identical in these characteristics, but one is religious while the other is secular, the religious person will still be 13 percentage points more likely than the nonreligious person to say he or she is very happy."[1]

What is even more revealing is that the people who are the least happy are those who never make a decision, those who don't choose, those who refuse to "pick a team." Brooks calls these people "the group in the middle." They might call themselves "agnostic," a person who states, "I believe in God but I will not choose one system." Brooks points out, the group in the middle is also made up of people who claim a specific faith but do not practice it. The group in the middle takes no action to increase their spiritual connection with an identifiable God. So, you have the religious, those who follow a "traditional" God – YHVH, Jesus, Mohammed, Buddha, a group with a system, a discipline, a practice. And you have its opposite, the "secularists," as Brooks labels them, the group without a god and, by default, are their own god because they decide to live a life based on their understanding of what is "good" and what is "bad or evil." Some might even label this group "atheists."

The research tells us, "People in this middle group are, toward the end of their lives, much more afraid of death than their counterparts in both the religious and secular groups. This suggests *people suffer when they think their actions are inconsistent with their beliefs.* If you believe in the afterlife and practice your faith, you will be secure in your future. If you have no faith and thus

---

[1] Ibid, p.44

have nothing to practice, you don't fear the consequences of your life. But if you have faith but don't practice it – look out."[1]

I added the emphasis because inconsistency between one's thoughts and words and one's actions is essentially why people reach a point in their lives which we label "the mid-life crisis." This is when they choose either happiness or despair. The happiness route is the work involved to increase IQ and EQ and, thus, peace, love, freedom – happiness. The despair route that is easier to choose leads to the opposite. When the first and less traveled road is chosen, a mid-life crisis can happen if the GQ is not added to the equation. This means if you want to be happy, be consistent. Be congruent. Your walk must match your talk. Either choose a god and a system to follow and practice or reject any religious or spiritual system. Inconsistency – waffling, debating, and never acting on what you profess to believe – is the worse route to take.

I recommend that everyone gets busy surrendering to and following, a "traditional" god and system. Quit the debate club. Choose a God outside yourself or claim you are the "One With Whom the Buck Stops". Make a decision, but do not hang out in the middle.

Disciples of Yeshua are warned to avoid the dangerous path of indecision.

> But let him ask in trust, doubting nothing; for the doubter is like a wave in the sea being tossed and driven by the wind. Indeed that person should not think that

---

[1] Ibid, p.45

he will receive anything from the Lord, because he is double-minded, unstable in all his ways. (James 1:6-8)

"These people worship me only with their words. They honor me by what they say. But their hearts are far away from me. Their worship doesn't mean anything to me. They teach nothing but human rules that they have been taught. (Isaiah 29:13)

"I know what you are doing. I know you aren't cold or hot. I wish you were either one or the other! But you are lukewarm. You aren't hot or cold. So I am going to spit you out of my mouth. You say, "I am rich. I've become wealthy and don't need anything." But you don't realize how pitiful and miserable you have become. You are poor, blind and naked. (Revelation 3:15-17)

"No one can serve two masters at the same time. You will hate one of them and love the other. Or you will be faithful to one and dislike the other. You can't serve God and money at the same time. (Matthew 6:24, Luke 16:13)

Choose! The words that come out of our mouth bring life or death. The world likes the gray area of indecision. It seems easier to be "agnostic" because you don't have to decide. But average thoughts are all about the gray. Great minds make a choice. If you never pick a team, you never seem to lose, but you also never have a shot at winning. Leaders want to win, so they decide. They choose. Pick a team and then ask the god you've chosen to help you structure your life accordingly.

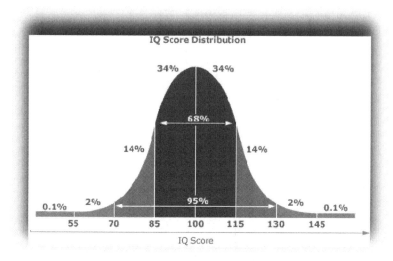

Why does the average person like the gray area? If we apply "The Happiness Formula" to this general area of questioning, we will examine some data (IQ) and then draw some preliminary conclusions to form a hypothesis. (EQ).

One thought is to look at the average IQ and what percentage of people measure "average"? If 100 is the average intellectual quotient of a human being, 68% of US citizens fall within 15 points on either side of the midline. We don't classify someone as "above average" until her IQ has risen to 115 nor do we call someone "below average" until her IQ drops below 85. An IQ above 130 is considered "gifted" and to be 30 points from the mean in the opposite direction, to have an IQ 70 or below is to be "cognitively impaired." (My name is Forrest. Forrest Gump.) Below 55 is officially "mentally handicapped" and above 145 is a "genius."[1] Therefore, 68%, what I call "the uber-majority" hang out in the middle intellectually.

---

[1] Various metrics exist which use different labels but the basic idea that 70% of the population as an average IQ is fitting considering 70% of anything is what we call "average."

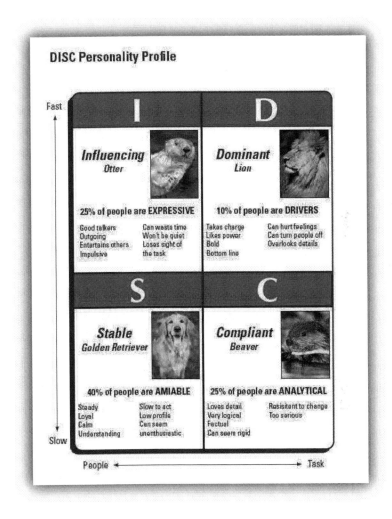

Another idea is to examine what personality tests reveal, considering EQ is more about your ability to respond and interact with others in the most effective manner possible and not necessarily about one's ability to learn. The DISC profile is a popular personality tool which centers on four different behavioral traits: dominant, influential, submissive, and compliant. While metrics vary, we find 13% of the US falls into the "Dominant" personality associated with the color red and the lion. 29% are labeled "Inspirational" or "Influencer" which is the color yellow and an otter. 35% are "Steady" which is green and a golden retriever. 23% are "Compliant" which is blue and a beaver. When you consider that the personalities of the steady and the compliant do not like change and resist leading anything, close to 60% of the U.S. population would rather give up the opportunity for gain or improvement because they have experienced loss and pain and hurt, and it is too distressing to consider the "risk" inherent in trying something new. The status quo is more emotionally safe. Once again, the majority hang out in the middle, emotionally and behaviorally.

I have kept a copy of and shared many times the 2005 article written by Seth Godin, "Change or Die." Godin discusses the research that reveals even in the face of imminent death, 9 out of 10 people will not make the changes necessary to save their own lives. The article continues this truth by citing medical research:

> Dr. Raphael "Ray" Levey, the founder of the Global Medical Forum, an annual summit meeting of leaders from every constituency in the health system, told the audience, 'A relatively small percentage of the population consumes the vast majority of the health-care budget for diseases that are very well known and by and large behavioral. That is, they're sick because of how they choose to live their lives, not because of environmental or genetic factors beyond their control...many articles demonstrated that 80% of the health-care budget was consumed by five behavioral

issues.' Levey didn't bother to name them, but you don't need an MD to guess what he was talking about: too much smoking, drinking, eating, and stress, and not enough exercise."[1]

The uber-majority would rather die than change. I have shared two other data sets to suggest the majority "hang out in the middle." This means they avoid decisions and action and they statistically are the least happy. Remember, the lack of action is a decision! So why is it so hard for people to change? Why will people settle for "average" or even possibly "below average" when evidence abounds in all areas of life proving, with just a little effort, they can make a huge difference in their peace, love, freedom – happiness?

People will change when they have a vision of the future that exceeds in emotional "payback," an outcome that overrides their deep-seated underlying beliefs. They must emotionally attach themselves to the hope that there truly is something better for them before they begin to take steps to change.

And now we are back to GQ. God and the system of belief people practice provide hope. A belief in a better future is the final element needed to make the changes and stay the course. It is faith and hope in God, the future, that gives one the power and ability to change. It is true freedom. It is divine!

The other side of hope is to accept that life was not created specifically for us. While we are uniquely and wonderfully made, the world does not revolve around us. We have to accept

---

[1] "Change or Die," Alan Deutschman. Fast Company, Issue 94, May 2005. P.53

that we have a role to play in God's world. This is what we were created for. We have purpose. We have a responsibility to work in the service of others.

In DeKoster's book, "Work: The Meaning of Your Life," he writes, "Work is really a divine institution and nor merely a necessary evil...work, indeed, gives meaning to life because it is the form in which we make ourselves useful to others, and thus, God...our work share in weaving civilization, which is the form in which others make themselves useful to us, by providing us with the tools for doing our work well...work sculpts the kind of self we are becoming through the choices we make in the handling of our talents on the job."[1]

"While the object of work is destined to perish," observes DeKoster, "the soul formed by daily decision to do work carries over into eternity...all of God's gifts to mankind are as a divine investment upon which the Investor expects full return."

Thus, to be infinitely happy, to reap the fullness of "The Happiness Formula," I believe we must recognize there is a price. That price is the same for anything that is great in life – responsibility. "From everyone who has been given much, much will be demanded; and from the one who has been entrusted with much, much more will be asked." (Luke 12:48 NIV) "Great gifts mean great responsibilities; greater gifts, greater responsibilities!" (Luke 12:48 The Message)

---

[1] Work: The Meaning of Your Life, LesterDeKoster. 1982. Christian's Library Press. P.x.

The uber-majority will settle for "good enough" or even "okay" because these standards do not require much. To be great is to participate in great ideals and actions. To be held in high esteem, one must do esteemable things which call us to love others first and foremost. To override self-centeredness is a requirement for greatness. We must pay the price of self-sacrifice; the cost of the Greatest Commandment (1) Love God with all your heart, mind, body and strength and (2) Love your neighbor as yourself.[1]

"To love" in Hebrew is "Ahavah" which has its root in the verb "to give." Nothing about loving others gives one room to claim anything for him or herself. Further, it does not work to follow up such ideals with, "But if you do all these things you will get what you want in the end anyway" because that is essentially a contract and not a covenant. A contract says, "You give to me; I give to you." A covenant says, "I will give to you

---

[1] Matthew 22:35–40 Then one of them, which was a lawyer, asked him a question, tempting him, and saying, Master, which is the great commandment in the law? Jesus said unto him, Thou shalt love the Lord thy God with all thy heart, and with all thy soul, and with all thy mind. This is the first and great commandment. And the second is like unto it, Thou shalt love thy neighbour as thyself. On these two commandments hang all the law and the prophets.
Mark 12:28–34. One of the teachers of the law came and heard them debating. Noticing that Jesus had given them a good answer, he asked him, "Of all the commandments, which is the most important?" "The most important one," answered Jesus, "is this: 'Hear, O Israel: The Lord our God, the Lord is one. Love the Lord your God with all your heart and with all your soul and with all your mind and with all your strength.' The second is this: 'Love your neighbor as yourself.' There is no commandment greater than these."
32 "Well said, teacher," the man replied. "You are right in saying that God is one and there is no other but him. 33 To love him with all your heart, with all your understanding and with all your strength, and to love your neighbor as yourself is more important than all burnt offerings and sacrifices."
34 When Jesus saw that he had answered wisely, he said to him, "You are not far from the kingdom of God." And from then on no one dared ask him any more questions.

no matter what." And that "no matter what" means I may never get what I want.

So are you ready for such love? Does this appeal to you? For the uber-majority, it does not. Even the disciples who walked with Yeshua during his three-year journey on this temporal plane struggled to understand and accept the requirement of "perfection" inherent in these commands. They asked Yeshua how many times it was required to forgive a person and when Yeshua replied with a response that essentially translated to "every time and always," they were aghast. Not only did it simply not make sense, they knew they did not have the heart actually to follow through.

Yeshua was the greatest manifestation of this unconditional love and forgiveness lived out. YHVH came to earth to give us an example of what this inexplicable, incomprehensible, ridiculous love looks like, and the uber-majority are still killing him for it. We can never manufacture this type of love, this type of sacrificial giving, no matter how much we develop our IQ and elevate our EQ.

Granted, this 100% surrender of self to a God who tells me that the way to life is through the death of self is not attractive. It sounds like a life of misery as people take advantage of me, use me, trample me because I am "dying to self" to give to them. I thought to be humble, selfless, and surrendering was not my style. Then I had my "burning bush" moment on Sunday, October 29, 2006. Until that day, my IQ, my EQ, my GQ was simply not ready to make that final leap of understanding. But when I did, it was undeniable, and everything changed.

October 29 is the day I claim as the birth of my spiritual self insofar as it is the day I finally embraced Christ as not just my savior but Lord of my life. I made a decision. I picked a team. I decided to stop sleeping with other gods, to end my adulterous ways. Formally, officially, unequivocally I signed a covenant. In 1988, when I accepted Christ, I signed a contract, "Keep me out of eternal pain, misery, despair, hopelessness – hell – and I will tell people I believe in Christ, but I "slept around" with all the gods because, heck, what if it doesn't matter. What if it as my mother taught and society reinforced, monogamy is not viable? In 2006, however, I finally chose one God to marry.

Bear in mind, from my accepting Christ as Savior to recognizing Him as God and Lord of my life was about 18 years of living life as I saw fit to meet my needs and desires. I was a woman who frequently said, "I will do what I want, with whomever I want, whenever I want, and wherever I want because I am in charge of my life. I make my own money, pay my bills, and short of something being illegal, I just might try it once." Whenever someone presented an idea that even slightly called into question my lifestyle choices, my belief systems, my idea of who I thought I was, I immediately defended myself with logic and rationale. After all, I had a documented "mentally gifted mind."

However, I had enough religious legalism under my belt to believe I might "burn in hell." So when I was a freshman at Stanford, and some Christians knocked on my door asking if I wanted to accept Christ, I happily prayed that Christ come into my heart so that I would have a place in eternal heaven. But I certainly was not ready to stop having sex with my boyfriend, drinking alcohol, cursing, partying, and generally "having fun."[1] I did not want to suffer for eternity either. If all I had to do was accept Jesus, heck, that sounded like a pretty easy admittance ticket to Nirvana.

While I appreciated that I had my ticket to heaven, I was not convinced he was the only One True God. After all, look at all the other super awesome systems of belief one could follow, and so many had been followed for millennia. Christ was cool with me, but He certainly was not "it," especially when you consider that the majority of the folks I knew who followed Him were judgmental, miserable and certainly not wealthy and rocking it on the "what do successful people look like" scale I wanted for myself. My litmus test did not have "spiritual superstar" as a criterion.

But like so many who hit their 30s and 40s, life stopped going as I had planned. Life stopped giving me everything I thought I deserved. Life stopped appearing so full of possibilities. So I began to study a bit more of the world religions and belief systems that people espoused made a difference for them. I recognized that I knew very little about the Bible and Christ and other world religions because I had not studied their writings thoughtfully enough. I had contempt before any real investigation.

---

[1] Why do we assume to have "fun" implies we must drink copious amounts of alcohol, have wonton sex, and otherwise, throw caution to the wind with our bodies and our minds. Simultaneously, people assume the life of a "saint" is boring. Why? More likely than not, if someone is this "saintly" they are usually highly controversial. More likely than not they live outside the accepted boundaries of society. More likely than not they fight a battle most of us would not. That doesn't sound boring to me; that sounds like a courage and strength I can only dream about.

However, when a mustard seed of humility arose within me, I figured out pretty quickly the "happiest" people were followers of a specific monotheistic system.[1] So, I began to study the major systems to see which made the most sense for me. I did not conduct an exhaustive search into the world systems, just those I could get access to via the communities they served in my area. If I was going to pick a team, I had to find a team nearby. I looked into all the various forms of "Christ" followers, (Catholics, Methodists, Church of Christ, Jehovah Witnesses, Mormons), the Muslims, the Jews, the Buddhists, and the New Age Unitarians were the systems I studied, the groups I visited.

New Age Unitarians and Buddhists do not have a specific god they can name, rather they emphasize a process to access a state of "enlightenment." All other systems had a pretty specific process to gain access to a named deity. As such, there is always the possibility that one may not "get in" if they somehow violated one of the many rules each group accepted and debated. It was because of this constant debate among believers that I knew I was in trouble.

Logically, if no one could agree conclusively without reservation which rules mattered, I didn't want any part of them. Furthermore, who would want a god who could cast you out if you violated one of the sacred rules? I was back to my

---

[1] Gross National Happiness, Arthur C. Brooks. 2008 Basic Books. P.43 "There is an immense amount of data on this subject, and it indicates conclusively that religious people really are happier and better off emotionally than their secular counterparts."

5th-grade Greek mythology studies which taught us gods are simply human constructs, which is why they are just as fickle and ever-changing as humans.

However, on Sunday, October 29, 2006, all my years of seeking and studying gods and religions and, specifically, my intellect, ceased. While listening to Pastor Pete Briscoe preach on Jesus as the Bread of Life (John 6:35), I viscerally felt and saw the holes of my soul close. I was finally satisfied! Before that day, nothing was "good enough" to satisfy my quest for The One True God. But after that day, I spent about a year on my knees, in tears, crying out to the God of the Universe. Specifically, I chose to call on Jesus. My IQ led me to this God system because in studying Jesus, I realized that not only could I never get "good enough," I could never get "bad enough." Jesus says that if I allow Him to be my one and only, I am "in"! No rules, no litmus test, no measuring up. Ultimately, I had to follow this system because it was the only one that acknowledged my EQ. It was not necessary to delude myself that I could "get worthy." Jesus let me know I already was. Thus, I decided to go for it.

Each year on the day of my spiritual surrender, I examine my walk as a disciple of Yeshua by looking through the almost 500 pictures I took during the two weeks I traveled to the Holy Land with the Briscoe family ministry, Telling the Truth. Almost every time I am struck by the power of God's truths revealed as He healed the man at the pool of Bethesda as well as how well it reflects my own story of resistance.

I was close to the age of the disabled man who protested when Jesus asked if he wanted to be healed.[1] I had logical reasons why I was not well. Just like the man, I was able to articulate multiple reasons why I was destined to be crippled. Ultimately, I was stubborn, and I was not engaging in the hard work of increasing my IQ and EQ because I had already decided the Christian god was a farce, an opiate. I had contempt, and I could not fully articulate why.

If there was an equivalent term for hating religion and God, without reason, like racism or sexism, I was this -ism. William Paley was a 19th century theologian and moral philosopher who defines a principle of all -isms, "There is a principle which is a bar against all information, which is proof against all arguments, and which cannot fail to keep a man in everlasting ignorance—that principle is contempt prior to investigation."

Fortunately, I was finally able to respond to what I was hearing. My EQ had finally increased enough that I was able to take action. However, like the man Yeshua healed, I had consequences of my past, the bad choices I had made that I had to carry with me. But I was healed! Regardless of all his protestations, this man eventually trusted the power of the God of the Universe to heal him, and so he walked.

Thus my walk as a Disciple of Christ began when I finally chose to believe the one basic Truth – to accept that Yeshua was the incarnation of the Almighty God in Heaven who made himself man to show us how to love others even while he struggled with temptations and broken humanity. And while

---

[1] Complete Jewish Bible, John 5:5-9 www.biblegateway.com

he had to learn and mature like all of us, he always chose to surrender his wants to God's will. More importantly for me, Yeshua supernaturally took on all my depravity, past, present, and future, and He made it clear it is not my ability to keep all the rules and laws or "must-dos" that would gain me my ticket to heaven, I will not have to work on what he already prepared for me in advance, a place in his home. As long as I asked to belong to his eternal, spiritual family line, to be grafted into the Vine, I would be eternally free.

I chose not to raise any more protestations or argue for all the "evil" I was still actively engaged in. I simply chose to believe that the God of the Universe loved me in spite of me and He always would no matter what. I could not get good enough for Him, and I could not get bad enough. He loved me and wanted to give me everything! Period. Now, this was a God I liked and could believe in, so I did!

In discussing how difficult it is to see God amid the daily ups and downs of marriage, Skip Moen in his book "Guardian Angel," addresses what the story of God, Jesus, the Bible is all about:

> It's a very good thing the Bible is not a book about ethics. It is not a handbook for positive thinking and wonderful living. It's not a Boy Scout manual or a ten-step self-help book. It's a book about *God's point of view*. It's a book about fallen people in a fallen world struggling to live a redeemed existence. It is a hardcore, down-and-dirty story about *God's fidelity* and our screw-ups. Nearly every hero of biblical proportion is, at the core, a tragically fallen person. Without God's

intervention, we wouldn't give them a second thought. That is exactly like you and me....[1]

So, did I choose Christ because I was convinced he was the One True God Above All Gods, King of Kings, the Alpha and the Omega, The Past, Present, and Future? I chose Yeshua because he had no rules, no test, no application to access him. He was the only God I found who seemed to be okay with me being me no matter how many times I messed up, no matter how ignorant my thoughts and beliefs. He loved me because He made me. He was the only God I found that had already invited me in and I didn't even know it. As I have worked on my relationship with Christ, my GQ has increased exponentially and, as such, so has my HQ.

So what does this mean for you? Are you supposed to accept Christ as your Lord and Saviour? I would be thrilled to show a new brother or sister their eternal throne room. But that is not the point of this book or the GQ element of "The Happiness Formula." Research proves you need a God, you need a system, and you need to follow, practice, and do the system. So, my advice – pick a team!

Find a God system you feel comfortable getting to know and dive in! Read your sacred texts. Learn your original language. Fellowship with those who claim the same god. Develop a relationship with this god and proudly proclaim you have found your spiritual life partner. Just as it is not my job to convince you to enter into covenant with Jesus, I do not mince

---

[1] Guardian Angel, Skip Moen. www.skipmoen.com p.124

words when I declare I have married Jesus. Order matters — faith, facts, feelings.

True happiness is reserved for those who make decisions and follow through on those thoughts. If you have chosen well, peace, joy, and freedom are the only possibilities. However, the fruit will either be sweet and nutritious, or it will taste bitter and provide no satiation. Either way, you will have evidence in this finite phase of your existence that you have either chosen correctly, or you need to course correct.[1]

It is fitting that I share the final words of the 12-step recovery program as defined by Alcoholics Anonymous:

> Our book is meant to be suggestive only. We realize we know only a little. God will constantly disclose more to you and us. Ask Him in your morning meditation what you can do each day for the man who is still sick. The answers will come if your own house is in order. But obviously, you cannot transmit something you haven't got. See to it that your relationship with Him is right, and great events will come to pass for you and countless others. This is the Great Fact of us.
>
> Abandon yourself to God as you understand God. Admit your faults to Him and your fellows. Clear away the wreckage of your past. Give freely of what you find and join us. We shall be with you in the Fellowship of

---

[1] "The fruit of the Spirit is love, joy, peace, patience, kindness, goodness, faithfulness, humility, self-control. Nothing in the Torah stands against such things." (Galatians 5:22-23)

the Spirit, and you will surely meet some of us as you trudge the Road of Happy Destiny.

May God bless you and keep you – until then.[1]

[1] <u>Alcoholics Anonymous</u>, 1929 Alcoholics Anonymous World Services, Inc. p.164.

CHOOSE WELL

To understand the importance of diving into the language, sacred text, people of your God-system, I have to draw upon the system I have used, that of the Jewish God YHVH as manifest in Yeshua and understood through the stories of the Bible. Remember, the idea is to emphasize the interplay of "The Happiness Formula" and encourage you to apply this Formula to your life and the God of your choosing.

The Bible is called "The Infallible Word of God." I have come to accept this as true because the more I understand the heart of God, the more I begin to Trust in what I have experienced that exceeds my talents and abilities. The more I dive into His Word, so much of what once appeared as heartless and punitive and even illogical, now makes perfect sense. Specifically, I now read the Bible knowing the writers are Torah observant, Jewish men from the 1st century and I study their language, Hebrew.

Hebrew is a language of action. Every Hebrew word has its root in a verb and as such, followers of the Jewish God, YHVH, who made himself manifest as man, Yeshua HaMashiach, understand that one must act her way into right thinking. "Hebrew verbs stress action and effect rather than just mental activity."[1] God's design is for humans made in His image to work, to do, and it is in the doing one shapes her heart and mind into a vessel for God's Perfect Purpose. Without the recognition that the goal of the action is to increase the

---

[1] "Walking in the Dust of Rabbi Jesus," Lois Tverberg (2012) p.37

connection between God and human, one is left to acknowledge something "less than" as the creator all the blessings and this something (an "idol") will always fall short of perfection.

So when I read the Torah and believe it is an antiquated system of rules that no longer apply, I miss the purpose, the goal of the behavior God is attempting to encourage us to practice. The God of the Universe knows that as we participate in a specific action, we will develop the mind (IQ) and heart (EQ) that is required if we truly want to know The Great I am more intimately and thereby, experience happiness.

When we apply our IQ to study the Hebrew meaning of "commandment," (mitzvot) a very different response will occur for someone who has a developed EQ. "Mitzvot" means "Divine commandments; a good deed or religious precept." The word mitzvah stems from the root tzavta = attachment. This tells us the mitzvah's purpose is to create a bond between G-d who commands and the man who performs[1] to increase the attachment (elevate your HQ). That started to make more sense even to someone as rebellious as I was at the beginning of the journey.

Performing "mitzvot" is akin to showing someone your love and respect through your actions, as opposed to using only words with no deeds attached. A rational, healthy adult with even a modicum of EQ will recognize the value of actions over words when it comes to expressions of the heart. Ask someone to define love, and they will talk about actions and other

---

[1] www.studylight.org/dictionaries/ckb/m/mitzvot.html. 2012.

tangible and quantifiable examples. We know we do not have to listen to what someone says they feel. We can watch their actions to learn everything we need to know about them.

In modern Western society, however, we elevate the mind over actions. "I think therefore I am," is the reason we value academic pursuits over other activities even while we admire physical achievement or volunteer activities. In God's universe, however, the idea that how you act reveals who you are is based in the belief that you exist not because you think but, rather, because God made you for His purposes. So what do your actions reveal about your character?

The God of the Universe teaches us "actions matter." Via thousands of pages in His love letter to us called the Bible, we read stories from thousands of years of a group of people he specifically trains up in His ways. Their lives are an example of what life is like, depending on your choices. Actions have consequences. Justice will be served.

Science confirms this truth insofar as energy is not lost; it merely transfers systems or form. New age religion likes to call this "karma." What you put into the universe will come back to you in some form or fashion at some point in time. We all are subject to "judgment" according to our actions whether we must pay the penalty in this time and space or the next. We all will answer and be held accountable for what we have sown into the world. It is so perfectly logical and scientific it is sometimes shocking to me that I fought this idea for so long and, yet, I was immersed in the scientific method for decades as a scholar.

Part of the reason it is so hard for people to grasp the foundational principle of energy is not lost as it relates to character, their soul, eternity, is because "the road to hell is paved with good intentions." The path to destruction is a slow, almost imperceptible slope downward and it is only when something fairly tragic occurs that one will wake up and notice they are "suffering" because of a series of choices they made. Further, those with low EQ will tend to paint the sins of others as that which needs to be brought to the light and for justice to prevail while they will gloss over their sin, defects of character, and ugliness with a paint stroke of compassion and forgiveness.

A healthy, mature person will see the patterns – a process of applying IQ to one's life – and course correct sooner than later – a process of applying EQ to one's life, unless of course, they are not healthy and mature, in which case, they will very often need to conduct more "research" by continuing in whatever behaviors, attitudes, and actions that got them to a place of pain in the first place, thereby experiencing more of what they already had. ("Insanity is doing the same thing over and over again and expecting different results.")

In the 12-step of recovery, it is taught "pain is the touchstone of all spiritual growth." Until such time the losses are so great one is forced to course correct, i.e., deterioration of health, loss of jobs, destruction of relationships, estrangement from friends and family, one will not usually begin to incorporate GQ and seek the help of others.

The Jewish community studies the Torah on a 52-week cycle. They call these weekly studies from Genesis through

Deuteronomy, parashah. During Parashat Ki Tavo ("when you come"), Moses continues a long speech in which he gives the new Jewish nation their final "instructions" before they enter the Promised Land. He starts with describing how each is to express his gratitude toward YHVH for all God has provided by defining the ritual of "first fruits." In today's (mis) interpretation of God's Word, we understand "first fruits" as giving 10% of our income to a religious institution.

When you read Deuteronomy 26: 1-11 one might be tempted to gloss over it assuming it has nothing to do with us in the modern age because (1) there is no temple at which to make an offering, or (2) we are not farmers, or (3) if you call yourself "Christian," this is the "old" covenant, and we are under the "new" covenant. (Again, another misinterpretation considering the Bible is <u>one</u> book, <u>one</u> story, <u>one</u> covenant.) Whatever the excuse, one can easily miss God's heart for us which is to mold us more into His image by having us do that which will allow for this transformation to occur. As such, this Parashat drives home the truth that if you fail to express gratitude and joy (because He made us for His purposes) and to show it in your actions, the descent (return) to bondage (hell) will begin.

[10] Therefore, as you see, I have now brought the first fruits of the land which you, *ADONAI*, have given me.' You are then to put the basket down before *ADONAI* your God, prostrate yourself before *ADONAI* your God, [11] and take joy in all the good that *ADONAI* your God has given you, your household, the *Levi* and the foreigner living with you. (Deuteronomy 26:10-11)

113

Because we miss the intended purpose, we do not obey/do/give thanks. Because we do not obey/do/give thanks, we miss the peace, the freedom, the happiness that God wants to provide in abundance.

"If you listen closely to what *ADONAI* your God says, observing and obeying all his *mitzvot* which I am giving you today, *ADONAI* your God will raise you high above all the nations on earth; and all the following blessings will be yours in abundance — if you will do what *ADONAI* your God says. (Deuteronomy 28:1-2)

So what happens when we have ignored God's handprint in our lives? What happens when we forget that we were once in bondage and set free, not due to any "good behavior" on our part, but rather because of God's love for us?

Curses = barrenness, fruitlessness, purposelessness, uselessness.

[47] Because you didn't serve *ADONAI* your God with joy and gladness in your heart when you had such an abundance of everything. (Deuteronomy 28:47)

> "You are free to make your choices but you are not free to choose the consequences."
>
> **Proverbs 4**
>
> **www.kasandravitacca.com**

At AlephBeta.com Rabbi Foreman creates videos to understand Torah. In discussing Parashat Ki Tavo ("when you come") which he carries over into Parashat Netzavim ("standing"), he states that when someone strays from the connection between their Creator and themselves, doubts arise and the insidious descent begins:

> He is the recipient of undeserved bounty, what if he fails in what the Torah asks of him? What if he can't be thankful? What if he can't share by giving of his time, talents and treasures to others? What happens then? Then your only way out of the guilt of your undeserved, wonderful circumstances is to lie to yourself and convince yourself that you do deserve this. Once I start getting used to thinking that I deserve stuff that I don't, I start losing my bearings; I no longer trust my intuitive sense of what I deserve and what I

don't deserve. I don't know the difference between the two anymore.

Now I look around, I see stuff I don't have, and I wonder to myself, do I deserve that too? Why don't I have that? That extra property over there doesn't feel so different than the property I already have, and suddenly I'm resentful, why don't I have that? How come he's got a bigger house than me? I'll move over the property marker. How come I got stuck in this relationship? Oh, I'll have a secret, intimate encounter with that forbidden person over there. I'll get what's due to me.

How did he get that way? I want to suggest the Torah's answer is he is just the third link in this chain. It all boils down to a choice you make.[1]

Each has a choice. Depending upon where he is with "The Happiness Formula," he may end up slowly sliding down the slope of rationalization and justification until he ends up secretly doing that which he never thought he could/would or maybe even wanted to do in the first place – he is in bondage – he is in hell.

Rabbi Forman's final words of encouragement to us in the Parashat are:

In the end, it's nothing less than a recipe for how happiness can be pursued. Have the courage to

---

[1] Parashat Ki Tavo, "What Does the Bible Say About Happiness." www.alephbeta.org

recognize undeserved good fortune and have the
generosity of spirit to thank the Almighty for it and to
share your bounty with those whose position in life is
less privileged than your own.

I was born in a prosperous time. I understand the
privileged position that history has placed me in.
What I have is a gift, and I must share it.[1]

Laws (rules, systems, boundaries) are meant to teach us values.
The tangible and practical has a spiritual reality. Laws allow us
to touch and feel the amorphous, ephemeral Truth and
Holiness of God.

But regarding anything beyond this, dear friend, go
easy. There's no end to the publishing of books, and
constant study wears you out, so you're no good for
anything else. The last and final word is this:
Fear God.
Do what he tells you.

And that's it. Eventually, God will bring everything
that we do out into the open and judge it according to
its hidden intent, whether it's good or evil.
(Ecclesiastes 12:13-14 The Message)

Your blessings or curses are a direct result of your choices.
Nobody makes you "do" anything specifically. Nobody makes
you "feel" any specific way. While we are a reflection of the
five people and/or institutions with whom we spend the most

---

[1] Parashat Netzavim, "The Pursuit of Happiness." www.alephbeta.org

time, in the end, you make decisions for you and, as such, you are responsible for everything that occurs in your life.

Choose well.

YOU TOO HAVE SUPERPOWERS

Our favorite protagonist pops up across all genres of literature, both classic and contemporary, in movies, plays, almost any story around the world for centuries – the HERO. The hero is after some ultimate objective and must encounter and overcome obstacles along the way to achieving this goal. He or she is usually morally good, though that goodness will likely be challenged throughout the story. Heroes' ability to stay true to themselves despite the trials they must face is what makes them heroic. That and the fact that they are often responsible for saving a bunch of people (or hobbits, or wizards, or space aliens).

While there are many types of heroes, we have a particular affinity for the "reluctant" or the "unlikely" hero because us "mere mortals" can relate better to the character who does not seek glory nor does he try to save the world but he ends up doing both. For example, Spiderman is considered one of the most popular and commercially successful superheroes because his character looked like us. Peter Parker, a high school student from Queens, was the regular guy behind Spider-Man's secret identity, and he dealt with rejection, inadequacy, and loneliness.

We all want to be the type of person who may not appear to be a bad-ass and might even take some flak for not flaunting our prowess but, watch out, if you push too far, which usually entails threatening or even hurting another, that is when you

119

will see our power. That is when we will change from Clark Kent to Superman or awkward high schooler to Spiderman or random Home Depot worker to The Equalizer or Security Guard to being Unbreakable.

It's why we favor the underdog in sports and the more true the story, the better. It is why the story of Daniel Eugene "Rudy" Ruettiger who did whatever it took to become a college football player at the University of Notre Dame resonates so deeply with so many. A poor, working-class immigrant, Francis Quimet, won the US Open in an era when golf was a sport only for the wealthy. The movie "The Greatest Game Ever Played," tells the story. Our heroes look so much like us. We want them to; we need them to.

We want to believe it is possible for us to overcome the odds stacked against us, real or perceived. We want to believe that we will persevere no matter the adversity because we have the tenacity and fortitude of character to stay the course no matter the cost. **We want to be a better version of ourselves. We want to be our own heroes.**

This is the goal of "The Happiness Formula."

ONCE YOU BECOME FEARLESS, LIFE BECOMES LIMITLESS.

www.kasandravitacca.com

Happiness is a temporary state when one seeks it for itself. But abundant peace, joy, love, freedom—happiness—is possible when we accept day after day, month after month, year after year the process of "The Happiness Formula." If you execute attitudes, actions, and behaviors applicable to each area, you will drive up your happiness quotient. Better yet, you will sustain it!

Ultimately, you are designed to be the master of own life. The Master of the Universe has given you all tools and resources to make that happen, and it is the tri-fold process of:
(1) IQ – seeking knowledge, using your brain, thinking,

(2) EQ – applying insight, behaving according to what you have learned, taking action, and

(3) GQ – trusting God with the results, letting go of the outcome, aligning yourself with those who honor the same process.

When you study the people, who are most successful, healthiest, wealthiest, emotionally most satisfied, the heroes of real life, you will discover people who have the "superpower" of controlling their emotions, marshaling their lusts, delaying the fulfillment of their desires. They exercise patience and self-control, fruits of the spirit which lead to love, joy, peace – happiness.

In the late 1960s and early 1970s, psychologist Walter Mischel, then a professor at Stanford University, conducted "The Stanford Marshmallow Experiment." It was a series of studies on delayed gratification. In these studies, a child was offered a choice between one small reward provided immediately or two small rewards if they waited for a short period, approximately 15 minutes, during which the tester left the room and then returned. (The reward was sometimes a marshmallow, but often a cookie or a pretzel.) In follow-up studies, the researchers found that children who were able to wait longer for the preferred rewards tended to have better life outcomes, as measured by SAT scores, educational attainment, body mass index (BMI), and other life measures.[1]

It is because this "skill" – self-control, patience – is so powerful, it is the foundation of EQ. EQ is "The Happiness

---

[1] You can read the actual study in various forms but it is so much more fun to watch a video. https://youtu.be/QX_oy9614HQ

Formula" element which has consumed the highest number of pages in this book and many others. If you can control your response at any given moment, you will be like the Matrix and Equalizer who can slow down the bullets and stop all the actions so you can explore all the possible outcomes and respond accordingly. In so doing, you will not so much re-wire your brain insofar as you bypass the emotional prehistoric animalistic fight or flight brain area, but you will have given the input just a few more seconds to travel its path to the pre-frontal cortex which contains your rational logic center. It is an active, intentional process that you have to practice.

Part of increasing your EQ is to acknowledge the facts, what is real and true, IQ, and then respond accordingly. So if you can accept the Truth that you have no other way to see the world except through your own eyes, you will accept the Truth that you are ALWAYS biased first! EQ is what allows you to know that because all you know as "real" is your perception of an experience, then you will slow down so you can consider what other reality might be occurring. In slowing down, you admit to your innermost self that there is a high probability that you do not know enough, so you must ask questions even to have a shot at being helpful and "right." Behaviorally what this looks like is, you have to take an active, intentional interest in another by listening to what is being said underneath the words before you respond to anyone about anything.

Most people are too busy listening to their ideas in their head to listen to you. Increasing EQ requires you to listen first! Specifically, listen to gain understanding, listen to hear the similarities rather than all the differences. If you look for the differences, you will find them, and you will never relate. You will always feel different. You will always feel better than or less than. You will always be odds with the world and yourself. Therefore listen for the similarities and not the differences and then ask questions. If you want to ensure the most harmonious outcome you have to ask yourself, "Do I want to be right or do I want to be happy?" And, more importantly, "do I care about preserving the dignity and honor of this relationship?"

You must ask before you respond. You must gain clarity before you give your thoughts. It will sound like, "You have used the word X, what does that mean to you?" Or "I hear you say Y, is this what you have said?" At some point you can offer thoughts, not answers; you can share your perspective, your experience, your heart, "May I offer some thoughts from my experience?" And as you share, make sure to share according to "The Happiness Formula" such that you share: (1) IQ - what you have learned, (2) EQ - your feelings as you processed through it, and (3) GQ - how God was present throughout all of it.

As you engage in this process you will simultaneously run the mantra/prayer in your head, " Lord, please make sure My thoughts are Your thoughts, that I hear this person with Your ears, that I see and observe this child of Yours with Your eyes, that my heart has the love and compassion You have for this human created in Your image and, Divine Master, let me respond according to the message You want to convey. Your will, not mine, be done." And, the short version which I sometimes accompany with gestures, "Lord, head, ears, eyes, heart, mouth. You, God."

When you train yourself to invite the Divine into your world before any words are spoken or any action is taken, you will increase your HQ because you will live out "The Happiness Formula."

To tap into your superpower, draw upon the supernatural and access the power of God.

WE ARE SPIRITUAL BEINGS HAVING A HUMAN EXPERIENCE

Because this is not a theological book, I won't be able to dissect what is essentially one of the most fundamental queries of being human: Who are we at our core? Who am I in spirit? Am I inherently good or evil? Because we are spiritual beings having a human experience, we have to decide with Whom will we align our spirit?

Dennis Rainey is the Co-founder of Family Life, a subsidiary of Campus Crusade for Christ. Since the organization began in 1976, Dennis' leadership has enabled Family Life to offer families blueprints for living godly lives, marriages, and families in more than 109 countries around the world. My participation with Family Life began as my husband, and I practiced "The Happiness Formula" in our marriage by actively surrounding ourselves with couples committed to the hard work of increasing happiness in their marriage.

While we were at a place in our marriage that each of us would describe as "excellent," we understood that happiness is a process that must be practiced day in day out, month after month, year after year. One way we chose to practice "The Happiness Formula" in our marriage was to attend a "Weekend to Remember Marriage Retreat" in February 2017. We signed up for the annual "Love Like You Mean It" Marriage Cruise for February 2018. By the end of the first day on the cruise, we committed to the next year's cruise. I also bought Dennis Rainey's book on the most critical choices you will ever make. Specifically, whether to choose a life with God or no God is the most important choice superseding all other life choices.

> "What we think about God really is the most important thing. And it's not just that other things will matter less in comparison; it's that other things won't matter at all. If we get this one thing wrong or, worse yet, neglect it entirely, life will be essentially meaningless. So if you want a life that matters, your quest for knowing God matters more than anything else."[1]

You are not just a physical entity; you are not just the rational, logical brain center. You, me, all of us are sentient, eternal energies which reside first in the emotional, feeling brain center. To come into the fullness of yourself as a human, as a spirit, one must study, get to know and then practice and act upon this spirit-self.

As I began to seek my answer to this fundamental question, I had to confront my biases, known and unknown. To fully grasp how to heighten and expand upon your GQ, you too have to confront your prejudices, your biases, your preconceived notions of God.

Because I am writing this book with Western culture in mind, specifically drawing upon statistics and research that mostly explore the first world reality of 21st-century people groups, I

---

[1] Choosing a Life That Matters, Dennis Rainey. Pp.14-15

am also operating from a "Christian" influence. I was not raised to believe in a specific god and was permitted to explore all realms of spirituality. I was raised with a stronger faith in the viability and excellence and "truth" of my brain over a "god" as defined by world religions. My world perspective is still that of someone seeped in the 20th century, dominant word power, westernized Christiandom.

One's worldview matters. To understand the necessity of increasing our God-quotient and taking actions to make that happen, we need a mustard seed of belief that GQ matters! Two thinkers, researchers, academics Lois Tverberg and Skip Moen have helped me understand more. I was introduced to their writings in 2015 when I joined a Christian led, women's group, focused on Torah and Hebrew. The woman who became known as my "rabbi" (it means "teacher), had been studying Hebrew for almost two decades. Like many of us "gentiles," she sought to gain better insight into herself by better knowing her Designer, YHVH via Yeshua, a 1st century, Torah observant Jew and what he might have "really" said and done during his brief walk in the physical realm. She asked all talmidim (disciples) first to read Lois Tverberg's "Walking in the Dust of Rabbi Jesus," and then, Skip Moen's "Guardian Angel: What You Must Know About God's Design for Women."

Tverberg's book begins by emphasizing that the reason I cannot understand a person "until I have walked in their shoes" is that I have no idea what their cultural world perspective is. I have no idea how they view humanity in this time and space. It is not just a variable of the fact that we come from a different part of the country or social class or speak a

128

different language. It has everything to do with an entire paradigm that I had no idea could exist. I do not know what I do not know!

Tverberg quotes a pioneer in Bible translation, Eugene Nida:

> The Bible is the most translatable religious book that has ever been written...If one were to make a comparison of the culture traits of the Bible with those of all the existing cultures of today, one would find that in certain respects the Bible is surprisingly closer to many of them that to the technological culture of the Western world. It is the 'Western' culture that is the aberrant one in the world. And it is precisely in the Western world...that the Scriptures have seemingly the least acceptance.[1]

Tverberg expands on this idea of our Western bias and actual ignorance:

> Throughout history, people have lived in extended families, practiced subsistence farming, and lived under the shadow of slavery and war. And around the world, many traditional cultures focus their children's training on sacred stories and order their lives around religious practices. With our individualism, secularism, materialism, and biblical illiteracy, we in the Western world are the ones who have moved farthest away from Jesus' world. Could it be that we're the ones who have the most to learn?[2]

---

[1] Walking in the Dust of Rabbi Jesus, Lois Tverberg. Zondervan 2012. P.26
[2] Ibid, p.27

The reason Tveberg's work was paramount to read before Moen is because "Guardian Angel" is a deep dive into the language of Hebrew as understood by Yeshua and those who studied so closely with him that the dust he kicked up while walking with him landed on their clothes. In particular, Moen frustrates many Christians as he calls into question precious theology, precious identity, ideas, and beliefs that might be wrong! Specifically, people struggle with his understanding of Hebrew when examining how God created male and female. Moen writes:

> The Biblical Hebraic view of women is radically different than the current cultural view. The Genesis account stands in opposition to the usual Christian interpretation and the Hellenized Jewish practice. If we want to recover romance, rekindle respect, reignite real unity and release each other to experience God's plan, we need to take a serious look at the mystery in these opening chapters of the Bible.

What thinkers like Tverberg and Moen and the numerous writers I quote throughout this book share is a basic quest to understand without ego or hubris, without a hidden agenda, they simply seek truth. As such, when you read Moen's description of himself on his website, I am compelled to reply, "Ditto!"

> [T]he key for me is dialogue, not doctrine. I do not find myself shackled to ossified propositions from past philosophical dilemmas. I do hope to understand someday what God told His people.

130

I have only one purpose – to find out what the text says, that is, what it meant to the audience that heard it first, what it meant in that culture's paradigm. So I search anywhere and everywhere that the text takes me. That's all. That's enough. I barely have time for even this.

I am trying to find out how to live as a Gentile follower of Yeshua who serves YHVH. Along the way, I am finding that a lot of the forms of Christian theology don't fit the Scriptures I read, and that means I have to rethink things. But please don't call me a heretic unless I actually become one.[1]

All writing is an attempt by the author to solve a problem. But that does not mean they have found resolution. As such, as we delve into the answer to the most fundamental question – am I born good or evil – we have to recognize even this question is steeped in a Western paradigm of the preeminence of the individual and, alas, the individual is not what life is all about! At the same time, you as an individual only have yourself to manage, control, consider, and you must if you have any shot at being a better version of yourself so you can manifest all the unique excellence God has planned for, in, and through you. While it may sound a bit like "what came first, the chicken or the egg?" it has more to do with the unknowable truths of God.

---

[1] https://www.skipmoen.com/about-skip/ "A Brief Personal Statement About biblical Investigation"

So, when Moen addresses this very question via his online blog, "Paul, Augustine, and Addiction," we are reminded that with cultural emphasis on the individual we are either left 100% to blame because, after all, a person should be able to utilize his intellect (IQ) and will (EQ) to control himself. So we try even harder and get more and more frustrated. Or we go the other route and throw our hands in the air begging for mercy from the Creator of the Universe in hopes that something will change while we remain motionless. At some point, yes, you must "beg" the Creator for mercy as you do your part to harness the IQ and EQ He gave you because, in the end, it is a spiritual problem that will only be solved by increasing your GQ.

Moen elaborates on how our Western mindset has hurt our ability to achieve happiness:

> We should note that the idea of an individual person, necessary for the development of sinful nature, [am I

inherently good or bad?] could only arise *after* the development of Greek philosophy.

Greeks were independent and engaged in verbal contention and debate in an effort to discover what people took to be the truth. They thought of themselves as individuals with distinctive properties, as units separate from others within the society, and in control of their own destinies.

Chinese social life was interdependent, and it was not liberty but harmony that was the watchword—the harmony of humans and nature for the Taoists and the harmony of humans with other humans for the Confucians. Similarly, the Way, and not the discovery of truth, was the goal of philosophy. Thought that gave no guidance to action was fruitless. The world was complicated, events were interrelated, and objects (and people) were connected "not as pieces of pie, but as ropes in a net."

The idea that there is something wrong with me is a direct implication of the doctrine of original sin, including the idea that there is *nothing I can do* to fix this.

One consequence of spiritual deprivation is addiction, and not only to drugs. At conferences devoted to science-based addiction medicine, it is more and more common to hear presentations on the spiritual aspect of addictions and treatment. The object, form, and severity of addictions are shaped by many influences—

social, political, and economic status; personal and family history; physiological and genetic predispositions—but at the core of all addictions there lies a spiritual void.

It's safe to say that any pursuit, natural or artificial, that induces a feeling of increased motivation and reward—shopping, driving, sex, eating, TV watching, extreme sports, and so on—will activate the same brain systems as drug addictions.

No human being is empty or deficient at the core, but many live as if they were and experienced themselves primarily that way. Attempting to obliterate the *sense* of deficiency and emptiness that is a core state of any addict is like laboring to fill a canyon with shovelfuls of dust. Energy devoted to such an endless and futile task is robbed from one's psychological and spiritual growth, from genuinely soul-satisfying pursuits, and from the ones we love.

In a state of spiritual poverty, we will be seduced by whatever it is that can make us insensate to our dread. That, ultimately, is *the origin of the addiction process, since the very essence of that process is the drive to take in from the outside that which properly arises from within.* The sparser the innate joy that springs from being alive, the more fervently we seek joy's pale substitute, pleasure; the less our inner strength, the greater our craving for power; the feebler our awareness of truth, the more desperate our search for certainty outside of ourselves. The greater the dread, the more vigorous the gravitational pull of the addiction process.

It is no coincidence that addictions arise mostly in cultures that subjugate communal goals, time-honored tradition, and individual creativity to mass production and the accumulation of wealth. Addiction is one of the outcomes of the "existential vacuum," the feeling of emptiness engendered when we place a supreme value on selfish attainments.

If one of us falls, we all fall. If one of us believes himself unworthy, we are all unworthy. And if one of us recovers, so then do we all.[1]

In the end, the real question is, "Do you want to be well?" [2]

"The Happiness Formula" is designed to help you understand that abundant peace, freedom, love—happiness – is possible and sustainable if you will do you are part to (1) get educated, (2) put what you have learned into practice, and (3) leave the results up to God. At some point, you have to decide to stop participating on the debate society and accept that you are currently a finite being in a physical body and, therefore, you

---

[1] https://www.skipmoen.com/2018/09/paul-augustine-and-addiction/?mc_cid=ead0dd7aff&mc_eid=2d98e05103

[2] "Some time later, Jesus went up to Jerusalem for one of the Jewish festivals. Now there is in Jerusalem near the Sheep Gate a pool, which in Aramaic is called Bethesda[a] and which is surrounded by five covered colonnades. Here a great number of disabled people used to lie—the blind, the lame, the paralyzed. One man was there who had been ill for thirty-eight years. Yeshua, seeing this man and knowing that he had been there a long time, said to him, "Do you want to be healed?" The sick man answered, "I have no one to put me in the pool when the water is disturbed; and while I'm trying to get there, someone goes in ahead of me." Yeshua said to him, "Get up, pick up your mat and walk!" Immediately the man was healed, and he picked up his mat and walked." Complete Jewish Bible, John 5:1-9 www.biblegateway.com

have the potential for "good" and "evil." You will only rise above your base, animalistic and "evil" nature to access the power of "good" if you are plugged into a Source that allows the Supernatural to flow in and through you.

So, if you are waiting for the promise before you engage in the behaviors, you have it backward. Do the behaviors, and opportunities present themselves. Doors open; you will have choices. More likely than not, it will look different than you thought but you will exponentially increase your happiness!

"THE HAPPINESS FORMULA" PLAYED OUT IN MY LIFE

"What we fear says a lot about us, since fear is closely linked to what we value and ultimately worship. All the world is lit up with the radiance of God our Savior. Fearing lesser things blinds us to the truth of Reality and glorifies the realm of darkness. The world system is based on slavery to such lesser gods and fears, but we are to walk in the awe of the LORD God Almighty alone, and the light of his reverence overcomes the fear of this world. As the Gerer Rebbe said: 'If a man has fear of anything except the Creator, he is in some degree an idolater. For to fear is to offer worship to the thing feared, and this form of worship may be offered only to the LORD.'"[1]

"Hi. My name is Kasandra, and I worship gods of all kinds." When one enters any 12-Step program, she learns the unspoken rule of introducing oneself with the first name only followed by the specific addiction that program addresses. For example, "Hello, my name is Kasandra. I am an alcoholic." Hello, my name is Kasandra. I am a compulsive gambler." "I am a love-addict." "I am an over-eater." The introductions go on until you have covered approximately 100+ addictions as defined by the anonymous programs one can join.

---

[1] Hebrew for Christians post in Facebook group, June 5, 2018

Because I was not sure what specific program, what specific addiction I had, I learned very early on it did not matter. Every program followed some version of the 12-steps originated in "Alcoholics Anonymous" and all of which were designed to help me recognize, I was not God, but there was "a God who could solve all my problems."[1] Eventually, as I came to believe in a Power Greater Than Myself, a God of my understanding, I accepted Yeshua HaMashiach, the Triune God, and accepted that anything apart from God as a source of all hope, joy, peace, freedom, and happiness was simply a false god, an idol.

Until this revelation, however, I had NO idea how addicted I was to the lies of the world and the enemy such that I was such an egregious "idol worshipper." It was also then the words, "I am a sinner" took on a much less offensive and judgmental sound and I heard them for their liberating Truth. Yes, I could now see and accept all the ways I which had been and sometimes still am a depraved, reprehensible, vile, repugnant, deserving of nothing "sinner"! I could not get good enough to overcome my filth and, thereby declare myself "worthy" of an eternal life of freedom and happiness. I simply am not that good.

Similarly, I accepted the foundational Truth that I am designed to serve. I was created to serve.[2] I will serve something. Hence, what I serve is my master. This was the beginning of my understanding of "The Happiness Formula."

I began to practice the discipline of taking ALL thoughts captive and presenting them to the Lord first. No matter the

---

[1] Alcoholics Anonymous, Author…
[2] Work: The Meaning of Your Life, LesterDeKoster. 1982. Christian's Library Press. P.x.

issue, the moment, the feeling, I began to practice filtering everything through the following series of internal questions:

IQ – What is real and tangible about this moment? Where am I? What is physically happening at this present time? What do I know that applies to this moment? What facts do I have? What data and facts are being presented to me that I might need to ask more questions about? How clear am I on what is "real" and what might be processing through some emotional bias of mine and therefore my perception of what is happening?

EQ – How do I feel about this moment? What words can I associate with what is occurring right now as it affects my breathing, my heart rate, my body temperature? Is it possible to define 'why' I feel this way? Am I aware of past biases, hurts, habits, hang-ups, false beliefs this moment is triggering? What questions can I ask to gain clarity, so I do not react emotionally but, rather, respond with grace and aplomb such that I respect others and myself?

GQ – What might God be doing with this moment? Might God have a bigger plan and purpose that I cannot see or even comprehend? What if God's plan in this present moment is all about everyone else and I am only the vessel through which He pours Himself so that He is revealed to others and there is nothing actually "in it" for me'? He is the Creator, and He can do what He chooses with His creations, and I trust His Truth that He has plans for me, not to harm me, but for me to prosper and have abundant life.

And then the prayer would follow, "Lord, thank you for Your eyes so I can see this moment as You would have me see it. Lord, thank you for Your ears so I can hear what You would have me hear in this present moment. Lord, thank You for Your heart so I can feel what You would want me to feel in this present moment. Lord, thank You for Your mind so I can interpret and understand what is happening in this present moment in accordance with Your will. If I am to speak, speak for me, Lord. If I am to respond, respond for me, Lord. If I am to keep quiet, still my tongue, Lord. Your will be done."

When you consider it takes about 90 seconds simply to read those words, what I had learned was the wisdom of PAUSE, REFLECT, BREATHE, such that this minute and a half pause is really only a nano-second process of internal questions that heighten my happiness quotient because I will practice and process through The Formula first before saying or doing anything. In short, these series of questions might also be:
(1) IQ – Does it need to be said or done? Or, is it true?
(2) EQ – Does it need to be said or done right now? Or, is it kind?
(3) GQ – Does it need to be said by me? Or, is this my battle?

And while the seeds of "The Happiness Formula" had been laid as early as 2005 and I had begun to practice this protocol, this discipline, I had a LOT of learning, or rather, UN-learning to do. Specifically, I had to learn about this God dude who I was getting more comfortable calling "Jesus." Because I had not fully decided for a specific God, the full articulation of the words that would filter through my head as I began to examine myself in any given moment, would take a little longer to complete. I was on the GQ journey, but I had yet to pick a team, choose the God with whom I would commit my life and surrender my all such that I could release myself to "Your will be done."

I knew God had something to do with happiness, peace, joy, freedom, but I was still all about me, myself and I. No matter how "gracious" and giving I might be at any particular moment, I still had not fully decided to accept that I was PART OF a Greater Purpose and not THE purpose. I still had a lot of WIIFM (What's In It For Me) and I AAM (It's All About Me) that had to be worked out.

During the summer of 2005, I was introduced to a foundational, fundamental Truth that made all the difference. While it took me a few years for fully articulate this Truth, I understood that life is, indeed, black and white. Everything is a choice between "good or bad," "right or wrong," "yes or no," LIFE or DEATH."

Adonai Eloheinu placed in my life an angel with skin who spoke Romans 8:15 into me, and I had my burning bush moment. This dark-skinned, bright-eyed, wild-haired woman spoke in scripture. Everything that flowed from her mouth weaved God's Truth, and I felt this Truth penetrate the deepest recesses of my soul, "Kasandra, don't you know you are a child of God, so there is nothing to fear?"

> The Spirit you received does not make you slaves so that you live in fear again; rather, the Spirit you received brought about your adoption to sonship. And by him, we cry, "Abba, Father." (NIV)

141

15-17 This resurrection life you received from God is not a timid, grave-tending life. It's adventurously expectant, greeting God with a childlike "What's next, Papa?" God's Spirit touches our spirits and confirms who we really are. We know who he is, and we know who we are: Father and children. And we know we are going to get what's coming to us—an unbelievable inheritance! We go through exactly what Christ goes through. If we go through the hard times with him, then we're certainly going to go through the good times with him! (The Message)

Leadership programs, the military, our parents, programs of recovery all teach there is nothing to fear but fear itself so walk into that dark room my four-year-old child and climb into bed. Monsters do not live under the bed. When we get older, we are still afraid of the monsters even though we know they are not under the bed. We tell ourselves we have matured and figured life out and now "know" the real monsters are the humans all around us. But is that a better way to live? How is that working for you…really?

We are afraid of losing what we have (real or perceived), so we live addicted to the past and react to life as victim, blaming others or ourselves. Or, we are afraid of not getting what we want (whether we truly know what is best for us or not) so we live addicted to the future and react to life like a bull in a china shop demanding others behave as we believe they should. In either scenario, whether we are the victim or the tyrant, and usually we are some combination of both, we are not remotely aware of the GIFT of the PRESENT moment, and we miss

ALL that is real and viable and possible. Hence, in recovery, the acronyms abound:

EGO – Edging God Out
FEAR – Future/False Events Appearing Real
ODAT – One Day At A Time
HOPE - Hold On Pain Ends and Hold On and Pray Everyday
FROG – First/Fully Rely On God

When I was finally able to confront the fact that I lived in constant fear (worry, concern, lament, insecurity) of the future not evolving as I had hoped and planned, I was able to see how much I constantly meddled in and manipulated the present without actually living in the moment. Eventually, the consequences of my actions led me to my "bottom." It was this bottom, this worst of times, that marked the beginning of my ascent out of the hell I had been in for about a decade.

I entered recovery in the Fall of 2005. At my first meeting, I had a "burning bush" moment. I distinctly heard the voice of God state, "Welcome to church." Until that moment, I had spent a few years in groups of people looking for a "church home," a place where I could belong and SEE God. Unfortunately, humans are good at cleaning up, suiting up and showing up for a moment when they are "supposed" to look good. Usually, this is during one day a week many world religions set time aside as "God time." I could not reconcile the other six days. I watched them cut up, party it up, and self-indulge in ways that make me blush. It was darn near impossible to find a place with "real" people who discussed "real" life who did not try to convince you they were holy and righteous and good and who, like me, were FULLY aware they were despicable, self-centered humans just trying to clean up. But God, He allowed my behaviors to run their course and I hit my bottom which led to a solution – a 12-step program – which led me back to THE solution – God.

In the end, the goal of the 12-step process, the purpose as defined by the original "anonymous" program and for which all others model themselves is "to help you find a God of your understanding that will solve all your problems."[1] And so it did.

After a year of attending four to five meetings a week, working through the 12-steps, and learning to live life on a more intentional basis with regard to God's presence in everything, I attended a "traditional" church service on Sunday, October 29, 2006, and viscerally saw and felt the holes of my heart, my soul, my spirit close.

In 2005, I began the process to change my whole way of thinking. Within a year, on October 29, 2006, I accepted a God called Yeshua who until then I had fought with all the research, data, facts and stats I could find even to the point of ignoring and combating the data, facts, and stats that pointed to Him in the first place. In 2005, I changed what I put into my body from drugs and alcohol to bad food, too many men, and far too many ineffective beliefs and outright lies. In 2006, I began my journey to a new me. I became a new creation as promised by Adonai Eloheinu and I desperately clung to His Truths until such time that I no longer felt desperate but empowered!

---

[1] Alcoholics Anonymous, Author...

It was this empowerment that enabled me to keep going as I dealt with the wreckage of my past. Specifically, I was in an abusive relationship which crashed and burned the same month I accepted Christ. It would take years to rebuild myself emotionally, financially, spiritually and it was often painful and dark and scary and lonely, and I was a mess! But I had "The Formula" even if I did not have the full name yet.

I was working "The Happiness Formula" in all areas of my life because I chose to believe His truth, His promise, that He did not come to judge, but He came so we might have abundant life.[1] I wanted to live in abundance, freedom, peace, joy. I wanted to be happy! I had the data, facts, stats, research, patterns, information of His Divine Truth as I was learning it via His Word, the Bible, (GQ). This was coupled with the data, facts, stats, research, patterns, information of what experts in neuroscience, psychology, human dynamics could reveal (IQ). I was doing my part to change behaviors that led to less effective outcomes for me and others (EQ). And, slowly, the smoke began to clear, and the dust began to settle, and I could see the light at the end of the tunnel.

From 2005-2010, I had a rebirth. I was a "new creation" and I was learning to walk in this new Kasandra. I felt like Mary Magdalene who had seven demons exercised from her as I, too, had multiple areas of darkness that I had to work out of my system so I could finally claim my new identity. While the Lord tells us He will take our heart of stone and give us a heart of flesh so we can feel, see, and respond to the world as He

---

[1] John 10:10

does, accepting this Truth such that I actualized it in my daily walk, took a while to understand.

During the first few weeks of January 2010, another relationship came to a crashing end. I had done it again. I had chosen a man just like the abuser I had kicked out in 2006. While I took solace in knowing I had walked away after nine months and not four years, I was still a weepy, dejected, mess, fully aware that the problem was within me and not solely these men. We are who we attract, after all. I had to confront the facts, the Truth of my patterns and, hence, myself. If I had dated two verbally abusive men, what the hell does that say about me?!

A woman who I befriended just weeks before called me the day of the breakup, and while I tried to sound pulled together, she sensed it and queried, "You don't sound good. Talk to me. What's going on?" a question to which the only response is an immediate outburst of snotty nosed crying. She invited me to a Christian women's conference at which she was one of the main speakers. While I honestly could not tell you what Jennifer said or what any speaker said, for that matter, I will never forget the Truth she spoke into me during a break.

Jennifer grabbed my hand and focused her gaze so intently; I had to back up a little. Jennifer reminded me of Truths I had read about but had yet to accept into the sinew of my being. She reminded me of my True Identity.

I am GOD'S child!

I have already inherited The Kingdom!

When I feel, sense, believe there is a reason to fear, worry, fret, lament, I must remember I have a choice to claim my true identity as His child, a recipient of His DNA or to succumb to this moment of fear and to believe this world and the enemy are not already defeated. Just because I may not tangibly, physically exist in Yeshua's perfected eternity does not mean the victory is not already declared.

On January 11, 2010, the fullness of my identity became so crystal clear I knew my level of joy, peace, freedom – HAPPINESS – would never suffer. After all, "I am the Daughter of the Most High God. Holy, Righteous, Blameless and Pure. I am perfectly provided for, perfectly secure. Can't you see the crown on my head?"

She is so comfortable in her own skin, she can laugh today and has no worries or fears about tomorrow.
Prov 31:25

Tom Bilyeu is a filmmaker and serial entrepreneur whose empowerment blogs, and videos emphasize the ability to change one's life by changing the story one tells herself about who she is:

> Identity and values drive behavior, so if you want to make a change, you have to change your vision of who you are. You have to begin to tell yourself a different narrative and the narrative you tell yourself about yourself is everything. Every time we form a new opinion about who we are, we're right; not because our

opinions are based on fact or even shared by the people that know us best, our opinions about ourselves are correct because every time we believe something about our identity, it becomes our reality.

We are constantly subconsciously creating the reality of our existence, so why not create it consciously? If you had the opportunity right now in this moment, to create an entirely new reality for yourself, what would it look like? Which traits would the new you possess? How would you react under pressure? And how would you push yourself to learn and grow? How would you push yourself to grow and get better? That person you're imagining, they're worth becoming. Get to know them. Get in the habit of thinking their thoughts, of seeing the world the way they see the world. Because when you do that, when you get deep inside their mind, when you see things the way they see things, then you are really just becoming your future self.[1]

This is what I chose to do. I chose to be who God says I am and today I love all of me. I downright dig on the human being called Kasandra Vitacca Mitchell, and I am thrilled I get to walk the path God has designed uniquely for me. His will is being done in my life because I made the dramatic decision to change. One Day At A Time. One Moment At A time.[2]

---

[1] Tom Bilyeu www.impacttheory.com

[2] The Serenity Prayer: God, grant me the serenity to accept the things I cannot change, the courage to change the things I can, and the wisdom to know the difference. Living one day at a time, enjoying one moment at a time; accepting hardship as a pathway to peace; taking, as Jesus did, this sinful world as it is; not as I would have it; trusting that You will make all things right if I surrender to your will; so that I may be reasonably happy in this life and supremely happy with You forever in the next. AMEN

As such, I make the horse ready for battle knowing the victory is the Lord's.[1]

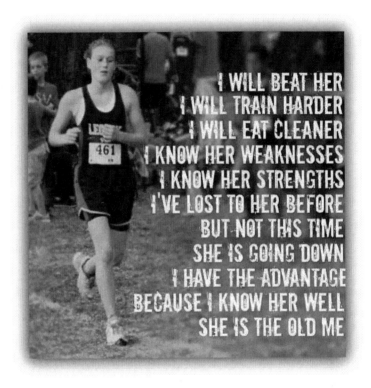

---

[1] Proverbs 21:31

BE YOUR OWN BEST CASE-STUDY

When we get into the habit of applying "The Happiness Formula" to every moment of our lives, we will discover we speak, act, and even feel "happier" because we will be engaged in the process that produces peace, joy, love, and freedom. Remember happiness is the journey, not the destination.

Along these lines, you will become your own best-case study. More to the point, you MUST become your own best-case study. We can only research life around us; we cannot conclude except in application to our own personal laboratory. While we pull data from others, we still work on the conclusions within ourselves.

You cannot rise to your highest self until you critically, consistently, methodically, scientifically, humbly observe yourself. This is the essence of "The Happiness Formula." I have become more comfortable honestly assessing what I know, how I feel, what I've done, what I want, what I believe, what scares me, what feels good, and what does not. This is an assessment of the data, facts, and stats as I know them at the moment. I can assess my feelings, wants, desires, hurts, pains, and fears in the moment but that doesn't mean I will be able to conclude anything. Very often I need to take time to think through all my feelings and weigh them against the facts and the Truth as I have come to understand it at that point in time of my life.

I am becoming more comfortable observing myself as best I can from the outside looking in. As I start to think of myself in third person, I will also begin to operate in the realm of the Spirit because The God of the Universe does not judge for the sake of condemnation but, rather conviction.[1] "For He knows the plans He has for you, plans not to harm you but for you to have a future and prosper."[2] Accordingly, He wants you to walk in the ways that will bring you to your highest and best self which means a lot of what you are thinking and how you are behaving might be revealed NOT to be effective.

Just because you can do something, doesn't mean you should. Just because something is legal, societally sanctioned, observed by the masses, does not mean it is ethical or even effective for YOU.

1 CORINTHIANS 6:12

- You say, "For me, everything is permitted"? Maybe, but not everything is helpful. "For me, everything is permitted"? Maybe, but as far as I am concerned, I am not going to let anything gain control over me. (CJB)
- "I have the right to do anything," you say—but not everything is beneficial. "I have the right to do anything"—but I will not be mastered by anything. (NIV)

---

[1] Romans 8: 1 Therefore, there is now no condemnation for those who are in Christ Jesus,

[2] For I know the plans I have for you," declares the Lord, "plans to prosper you and not to harm you, plans to give you hope and a future. (Jeremiah 29:11 NIV) I know what I'm doing. I have it all planned out—plans to take care of you, not abandon you, plans to give you the future you hope for. (Jeremiah 29:11 The Message)

- Everything is permissible for me, but not all things are beneficial. Everything is permissible for me, but I will not be enslaved by anything [and brought under its power, allowing it to control me]. (AMP)

1 CORINTHIANS 10:23

- "Everything is permitted," you say? Maybe, but not everything is helpful. "Everything is permitted?" Maybe, but not everything is edifying. (CJB)
- "I have the right to do anything," you say—but not everything is beneficial. "I have the right to do anything"—but not everything is constructive. (NIV)
- All things are lawful [that is, morally legitimate, permissible], but not all things are beneficial *or* advantageous. All things are lawful, but not all things are constructive [to character] *and* edifying [to spiritual life]. (AMP)
- Looking at it one way, you could say, "Anything goes. Because of God's immense generosity and grace, we don't have to dissect and scrutinize every action to see if it will pass muster." But the point is not to just get by. (The Message)

While our IQ is designed to identify data, facts, stats, research, and patterns without judgment, without agenda, without bias, it is our EQ that assigns value, worth, meaning to what we learn, observe, and identify. And, the Source we draw upon to determine value, worth, and meaning is, ultimately, our God.

We are called to work within the confines of our ability. And, because we can only work within the confines of who we are, becoming my own best-case study, practicing the liberating discipline of observing me from outside myself, requires the daily practice of surrender.

In recovery, this practice of surrender is summed up in one statement found in the preamble which is read at the start of every 12-step meeting around the world, "I had to let go of my old ideas absolutely, or the result was nil." When you use your IQ to analyze this statement, you realize "old" ideas are anything from yesterday. Even that which I thought a few hours before this moment, anything five minutes before having just read this sentence, is an "old" idea!

In all seriousness, to live in all that is real in the present moment, to come to an awareness of how anything you thought, said or did just seconds before is an idea and behavior you can change, is downright exciting! To come to this level of present moment awareness is what will enable you to pause just that much longer, so you can execute "The Happiness Formula" and get the most effective and joy-filled response from others and, specifically, yourself.

When I began studying Hebrew and Torah, I was blown away by the beauty of "manna." God chose a random, insignificant people group to use as His messengers for His love and to show us how to complete the image of Himself in us so that we can achieve a bit of "nirvana" in the here and now even amidst all the brokenness. It is through the story of these people and all the randoms they "adopt" along the way, an adoption which occurs when these "foreigners" claim YHVH as Lord and walk in His ways, that we learn how difficult the path will be and, yet, how faithful God will remain regardless of how we behave. Skip Moen addresses the unfortunate reality of seeing ancient peoples as somehow different from us:

> I don't think we know the people of the Bible very well. We are the victims of years of watered-down teaching. The stories of the lives of our spiritual ancestors have been sanctified. We know the triumphs of their faith, but we have little appreciation for the times of humility, disobedience, and failure. Of course, there are notable exceptions. We have heard of David's adultery and Samson's seduction. But most of the time, our attention is focused on the heroic acts, even if they come about as a result of sin.

> This myopia damages our identification with these people. We see them as something special, living beyond our meager spiritual capabilities. But if we look at the stories of their lives, we will discover something amazing. The Bible never glosses over the failures of people. It never avoids describing their disobedience. It never paints them as anything but completely human. There is a good reason for this. The Bible is not a book about past spiritual heroes. It is a book about God's faithfulness to His promises in spite of the failures of the human beings whom He chose as the messengers of His grace. The Bible is God's story, not ours. So, there is very little

room for hero worship, saints on pedestals or spiritual supermen.[1]

When we fail to recognize the very present humanity of these people, when we fail to understand they often had very little to no faith, when we fail to look for the similarities and only see the differences, we miss the beauty of their daily protection and provision. Our manna tastes bitter rather than its sweet potential.

"Manna" in Hebrew means "What is it?"[2] For forty years, the Israelite nation wandered in the desert as they sought to secure a home in the "Promised Land." God had just freed them from 400 years of bondage, and now they had to live the dry, parched, discomfort as nomads. And, yet, God provided daily. Their clothes and shoes never wore out, and they had protection and food every day without toil or labor. Their only effort was to gather the manna that appeared supernaturally each morning and prepare it for nourishment throughout the day. If they tried to keep a portion for the next day, it would rot. They were to collect what they needed for each member of their family. On the one day the Lord asked them to rest, the Sabbath, He allowed a double portion to be collected so they could indeed Shabbat.

Every person was given the same food, and yet not everyone experienced it the same. The flavor corresponded to how one received the gift – was one humble and grateful or entitled, believing they deserved such provision? Those who recognized the blessing inherent in the daily provision experienced the

---

[1] https://www.skipmoen.com/2018/09/history-and-story-1/
[2] https://www.studylight.org/lexicons/hebrew/4478.html

manna as "sweet as honey." For those who complained of their lot in life, blaming God and others for their present condition, the manna was described as bitter oil.

We, modern day, first world, Westernized people have the same struggle: can I accept this day as it is such that I conduct my work as needed? Remember, they still had to prepare the manna to be eaten. Can I accept that I must put in the work today without any guarantee that I will have a good future because of my efforts? Remember, the manna would spoil if one tried to save it to the next day. Can I have an attitude of innermost gladness knowing today is enough? Am I able to stay fully aware of the present moment? Make a conscious, intentional effort to examine yourself in the midst of daily events. Be your own best-case study. If you are honest, you will probably find the answer is "no" to these questions.

At the start of every day, I recognize that yesterday is gone, tomorrow is but a hope so today I will embrace the day with all the wonderful and glorious moments I GET TO (not "have to") participate in from the daily list of to-dos to the expectations of others to the demands of some. I will walk into this day with a fresh mind secure in what I know (IQ), willing to do what I can (EQ), and open to what God wants to reveal (GQ). In the end, I choose peace, love, joy, freedom – HAPPINESS – regardless of the circumstances. And, yes, the manna is sweet as honey!

So what does this process look like?

I have the honor of mentoring quite a few people, mostly women. Very often these women do not share a belief in the God I worship, and they even question the existence of a God.

However, it is never my job to convert them to follow any specific God. I share with others my experience, strength and hope in the system I have followed so all areas of my life, which I map out via an annual planning process,[1] are aligned with what I have learned, how I behave, and the beliefs I espouse. One of the first lessons I have to help others embrace is how to see themselves through the lens of a scientist, an academic, a researcher examining a case study. Like almost anything that is good and worthwhile in life, you learn via OJT – On the Job Training.

A text exchange with a 30-something will illustrate the point. Ideally, this real-life exchange will resonate either because it is what you experience in the here and now or, for those of us who are on the other side of this angst, we will humbly shake our head with knowledge and gratitude that we are on the other side of such discomfort:

> "I feel like I'm supposed to have identified which things are my God-given gifts and take risks and "live big" to help others. But that scares me, and I don't know if what I'm doing is right or not. And then, of course, I end up basing my decision of what is right by comparing myself to what other people are doing (which I know is stupid).
>
> Then not to mention that God is love which is what we are supposed to be in all situations and I know I'm sooooo far from that mark it's not even funny. Then I

---

[1] You can access the "Goals Wheel" on my website - https://kasandravitacca.com/applications/. I conduct online and live workshops on "Annual Planning" and "Budgeting." The tools are the site are a simple visual as well as a viable tool to begin the process.

realize I have so much work to do on myself and I don't even know where to start, and it's frustrating. Which leads me to believe I'm trying to live up to an ideal that is unattainable which is depressing because part of my personality is that I am an approval seeker.

And when I compare myself to others (like you or my husband for example), it seems like you have everything worked out and I never will."

Mikayla, my mentee, knows the importance of examining herself without condemnation because we have discussed the importance of gathering facts (IQ) and processing them through her emotions so she can continue with behaviors that benefit her and stop those that do not (EQ). Her text reveals her progress in expressing her beliefs and feelings which heretofore she could not and would not due to actual ignorance as to what is possible, as well as, fear to formally confront herself. In my response, I speak Truths I have learned as a follower of Yeshua and while Mikayla is not accustomed to such language and may not understand everything, "The Happiness Formula" works when one is open to the influence of a God:

I love you. You are soooooooo on the path of perfection. You are so "working out your salvation with fear and trepidation" which is akin to keeping your eyes on the prize and disciplining your body to run the race.

Our job, our purpose, is to run the race. Period.

The prize is the process of seeking His perfection lived in and through us and, alas, we usually don't get to know whether we have done "right" and done "well" except in hindsight. It's like this constant leap of faith daily. Truly. Daily leap of faith until you get comfortable being uncomfortable.

And, yes, comparison is a BEE-ATCH. Let what you see in others motivate you to want what you THINK they have, always remembering you have NO idea what the truth is; meaning, they may not have what you so admire. Similarly, let what you see in others as repugnant to you, be that which you seek to purge from yourself first rather than to condemn them for a perceived flaw on their part.

While perception is NOT reality, it is all we can take in and understand at the moment and, as such, it is as real as it is going to get, in the moment, which is why we have to pause long enough to consider:

(1) IQ – Do I have all the facts?
(2) EQ – Am I in touch with the emotions this moment is causing within me and can I identify these feelings without judgment and condemnation of myself or others but as a "flag" to highlight what the possible lesson is for me or others? And
(3) GQ – What might God be doing with this moment? How might God be in the details?

Mikayla's response brought home another critical truth of what this process will evoke – loneliness. Before your HQ can rise to the apex, it has been my experience it may fall as low as zero. LIFE is experienced through death. Until you are prepared to die to self, you can never experience the pinnacle of peace, joy, love, freedom – HAPPINESS.

I concluded my text response with, "Does this make sense?" to which Mikayla replied, "Yes, totally makes sense. I didn't realize the path would feel lonely and sad though." ... She nailed it! She was on her way. So I replied:

> Holy hell, girl, yes! Very very wildly freaking sad and lonely until you realize that absolute FREEDOM is found in this "loneliness" because, in the end, it, everything, all of this, that, and the other is about God.
>
> You and me, Big Guy in the Sky, just You and me. Period.
>
> No husband to please. No children to worry about. No clients to appease. No ideals to uphold. No pursuits to achieve. No actual goal or outcome. Just God. God.
>
> Sit in the space of that "loneliness." Sit in that feeling. Let it hit the deepest recesses of your heart so you can purge anything that will block its Truth. Know that as you sit in that space, you are surrendering to God and allowing Yeshua to fill you with Himself.
>
> When Jesus hung on that cross and supernaturally took on all the depravity of humanity past, present, future,

he had to descend to the deepest recesses of hell because that is where our reliance on and belief in what *we* create, what *we* control, and what *we* know leads us. And then he had to DIE to those things, for us, which is what you are feeling.

To be "sad" is to mourn, to feel the loss of something/someone. You are in mourning for the loss of your old self and that, my friend, is the pathway to peace. You must die to self to live in Christ. He did not come to condemn the world but to save it as He teaches us that to die is to live. To surrender is to win.

Do not run from these feelings. Let them flow. Let them hurt. Cry. Express them. And always thank God for them. I promise, as God promises, your tears will be turned to joy. Those who mourn will rejoice. The meek, the humble will inherit the earth.

You will overcome all that is in the here and now because He has already overcome it all. The victory has already been declared. You are simply walking into His reality so that you can live in His light in the here and now.

I so love you, Mikayla. I am so proud of you!

Becoming your own best-case study takes courage. You will be vulnerable. You will feel like you are "losing it." It is scary. It is uncomfortable. It is lonely. It is why so few do the hard work of applying "The Happiness Formula" to their life. In the end, it is why so few are truly, sincerely, in the deepest recesses of their heart and mind and soul, HAPPY.

Another reason becoming your own best-case study takes courage is because it doesn't end! You don't arrive. You don't graduate, get the diploma, finish the program, complete all the steps. You keep stepping, you keep learning and un-learning, you keep keepin' on.

Around 2012, I left active participation in my recovery group. My life has become full and busy and downright, wonderful. I prioritized other activities over this group. Specifically, I was a very active member in a local traditional church with many ancillary "bible study" groups so, heck, I didn't need the practice of the recovery discipline, so I told myself. By 2015, I was a mess! While I had not remotely slipped into the hell I had once descended, I was actively carrying around the shovel and looking for a place to dig. So I went back to my recovery group and started the step process again.

The good news is, working through the steps after having spent so many years prior in the committed practice of them, was a much "faster" process insofar as "muscle memory" kicked in, much like riding a bike after a while of not having done so. During that time, however, I had to confront some new insights about myself. Specifically, I had learned much earlier in my recovery journey that my first "drug of choice," my first real and persistent "addiction," was performance, achievement, work. "Hi, my name is Kasandra, and I am a workaholic." By 2015-16, the final release of this addiction was complete as evidenced by an extemporaneous message I wrote on January 9, 2016, to the woman who originally introduced me to the 12-step process in 2005:

> I am in a better space today. Just came back from a women's meeting. When I went to a recovery meeting a couple of days ago, a woman told me to write down my list of fears. Just write. So, I have done so, and upon re-read, I can see some patterns, but I need to share with a friend who loves me. Something about the list scares me. This sounds like a Captain Obvious statement considering it is a list of fears but something else – am I afraid to be afraid? Maybe that should be on the list? Anyway, I am not sure what is going on with me right now.

> I simultaneously feel like a mess and yet feel completely secure that God will work this out. It's His timing because, alas, this is all His. I am not sure I have anything to do with what is happening inside me right now. I have a deep sadness, but it's as if it is not me. It is as if something has died and I am in mourning? My cousin committed suicide, and that is just f-ed up, but it is not like we were best friends. She was always super nice to me, but she was seven years older, so we never hung out.

> I really really do not want to do my job as I have done it 1-on-1 with clients so maybe it's the death of that passion. Maybe it's the death of passion over a "job that must have passion" meaning, I sort of don't feel like I have the idol of work anymore, which is a GREAT thing, but work was my best friend my whole

life. It was ALWAYS my solution. I think about how recovering addicts speak about drugs and alcohol. They speak lovingly about it at times because it was their solution. It was never my main solution. BUT I relate to having idols so, heck I might be on to something.

Did I lose my best friend?

Dangit, I actually want to cry at that one. F-ing sick and wrong if indeed my greatest addiction is and was "work" and today is the first day I actually realize it. Really really realized it. A day I can admit to my innermost self that I am a workaholic and my life has become unmanageable. Wild! Totally f-ing wild.

Sometime in 2005-06, I accepted the fact that work had a stranglehold on my life. I looked at the data, facts, and stats of how my life had progressed up to that point and understood in an academic, scientific way of knowing that performance, achievement, work meant more to me than their intended purpose. I attached my identity to that which "paid" me either in awards earned, money paid, or accolades received. My IQ was in full operation, and I could "see" myself.

Yet, I did not "know" myself fully until 2015/6, a decade later after I had taken myriad actions and steps to change behavior and examine myself with honesty and humility over and over and over again. Then I could feel in the deepest recesses of my bones, to my soul, in my spirit, that I was NOT the work I did, the awards I received, the accolades I had earned. While my actions mattered, in the end, I was a Child of God fully

165

committed to His purposes. This was manifest in activities I engaged in daily mostly just to "keep busy" and, ideally, serve others. My EQ had caught up as I practiced increasing GQ in my life.

The heavens produce daily manna, and it is sweet and satisfying beyond the peace, joy, freedom – happiness – it provided yesterday!

When you become your own best-case study, you will learn to love yourself more than makes sense and more than the world can comprehend. It is precisely because of a love this true, this pure, this honest, this vulnerable, this REAL, that it is Supernatural!

LIVING IN THE TRANSITION, THE GAP, & THE AWKWARD DISCOMFORT

There is an interplay of the three elements, the dance of IQ and EQ and GQ, how we maneuver in a 3D reality between (1) what we know and have learned, (2) what we understand and chose to execute against or not, and (3) what is possible and unknown. This dance is what transcends time, it is where the eternal is found.

To operate in a world that is solely about what a finite human can take in and understand (IQ) and apply (EQ) is so horribly defeating and sad. It denies all that a sentient being knows in the deepest recesses of its being →we are NOT human beings having a spiritual experience; we are spiritual beings having a human experience. We live in "the Matrix," and the reason we can slow down the bullets is that there is another realm of existence that is only accessible when one recognizes s/he did not create this temporal space in the first place. There is A Creator who makes it all possible. Hence, life is more like the "The Shack" or other movies that try to give us a sense that a Higher Purpose a More Elevated Rationale and a Far Greater Love is operating.

So, to live in the transition, to live in the abundant happiness of "the gap," one must get very comfortable with the frequent discomfort of this temporal time and space. A discomfort that may arise every other minute one lives in the here and now. When you accept that your IQ and EQ will never reach the highest potential within you without the equal application of GQ, you are also accepting a life of frequent discomfort. We are IN the world but not OF the world. We are always sojourners in a foreign land speaking a different language, practicing different customs. Hence, get comfortable being uncomfortable because it is then you will find abundant comfort, freedom, peace, love, joy - HAPPINESS.

On Facebook one day, I came across a post of a young man I have come to love and respect for his vulnerability and authenticity. I met him when I enrolled my son in an acting and modeling program when he still a child and David Earl was one of the coaches. David posted:

On a plane. Looking out a window. Appreciating the view.

It's been an active summer. Lots of places. Backlogged on photos to share. Learning. Experiencing. Appreciating the seeds that have produced fruit I can see. Seeing opportunity for more growth.

In this moment, I just want to be still. To quiet the busy. My heart aches for something I don't see and can't put my finger on. I feel a desire to be home, but I don't associate home with geography anymore. Home is found within. And am not feeling it within or without. I feel adrift. Which is maybe why I've been feeling such a desire to be held.

I don't always understand the moment I'm experiencing. Sometimes I wanna drown it out. Other times I wanna look away. Distract. Run. Ignore. But I always know I'll come to the end of those and be back where I started. So, I try not to choose those anymore. At least not often. But when I do, I'm aware I'm doing it.

Right now, I feel like I'm looking at my moment. Not understanding all that I'm experiencing. Wanting to. Feeling. Observing. Wanting it to be different does no good. Resisting it doesn't. Just experience it. Knowing eventually, I'll see more clearly. Knowing discomfort always comes with an invitation and opportunity. Knowing that what can be shed will be shed. Till all that remains is true.

My heart feels like its ears are wide open straining to hear something it knows it needs to hear and understand. But I don't know what it is. It can feel very alone to sit in your moment. To be still. To listen to what's happening within. But it's good. The moment is all we have.

So, don't drown out or tune out of yours. Tune in. Dial in. Feel. Observe. Be present. Don't judge or label the moment. Experience it. You be in yours. I'm being in mine. It's all we can do. And it's good.[1]

If you want abundant comfort in life, if you want abundant peace, joy, freedom – HAPPINESS, get comfortable being uncomfortable! "Discomfort always comes with an invitation

---

[1] Facebook post chat September 15, 2018 with David Earl, Professional Model, Heart and Life Coach.

and opportunity." You are invited to use your IQ, what you know, what you have learned, your experiences, and as you filter this knowledge through your EQ to determine what do you want, what is possible, how do you feel about all of it, it is then you apply GQ to make a final decision for the moment knowing the future is not yours to know.

One of the most important lessons in life - one I believe most people never learn - is that almost everything important is a choice. We choose whether to be happy (or, at the very least whether to act happy), whether to be a hard worker, whether to be honest, whether to be kind, whether to see miracles, and, yes, whether to believe in God (or, at the very least, live as if there is a God).[1]

We make choices in the here and now that directly impact our level of happiness during this life. Only one choice affects what life looks like in the hereafter.

---

[1] The Rational Bible, Dennis Prager 2018

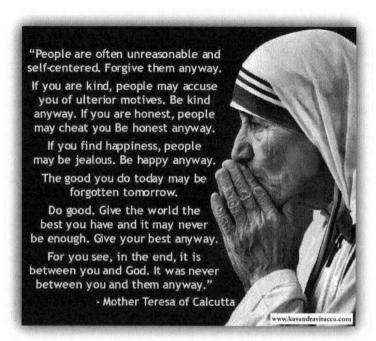

"People are often unreasonable and self-centered. Forgive them anyway.

If you are kind, people may accuse you of ulterior motives. Be kind anyway. If you are honest, people may cheat you. Be honest anyway.

If you find happiness, people may be jealous. Be happy anyway.

The good you do today may be forgotten tomorrow.

Do good. Give the world the best you have and it may never be enough. Give your best anyway.

For you see, in the end, it is between you and God. It was never between you and them anyway."

- Mother Teresa of Calcutta

www.kasandravitacca.com

HOW DO YOU "DO" HAPPINESS?

Up to this point in the book, we have read a lot of stories, processed research, and, depending on your brain, scanned far too many words. We live during a time when the average adult attention span has decreased to eight seconds. People do not want to read more than a list. Thus, the following chapters focus on various applications of "The Happiness Formula" in more of a list like fashion.

We explore it in application to a famous poem. I list daily "to-dos" that allow me and many others who have great success and joy in life to sustain a high state of happy. We dive into the importance of planning and the categories of an annual plan. We look at how "The Happiness Formula" applies to the three areas people seek the most help via books, internet searches, and professional consultants: health, wealth, and relationships, specifically marriage.

The final "formal" entry in this book (appropriately titled "Final Thoughts") is a bit more of my story and some somewhat tangential but ultimately cohesive thoughts on "The Happiness Formula." While I have weaved bits and pieces of who I am throughout this book, "Final Thoughts" is an attempt to provide more background for those for whom the God of the Universe might direct my way for more. As such, get to know me and feel free to invite me to speak at your professional associations, in your companies, at your social gatherings. Invest more time in learning and sign up for my online webinars. Tap into my expertise as a wealth coach and let's set up a consultative phone call.

Immediately following my "Final Thoughts", I offer prayers, one-offs, truisms, pithy statements that are simply too good not to share as well as words to music that move my soul.

However you choose to follow up, stay in touch! It is a deep honor to be of service to others and, specifically, YOU! I pray that you will continue to read and as you explore the rest of the pages of this book, "The Happiness Formula" blesses you in ways that transcend your understanding. I pray your spirit responds with joy and gladness became you know IT IS POSSIBLE TO BE HAPPY AND YOU ARE READY TO MAKE IT HAPPEN FOR YOURSELF!

"May God bless you and protect you; the Lord make His face shine upon you and be gracious to you; the Lord lift up His countenance upon you and give you peace." (Numbers 6:24-26)

May the God of hope fill you with all joy and peace as you trust in him, so that you may overflow with hope by the power of the Holy Spirit. (Romans 15:13)

I pray what God spoke to me, speaks to your spirit such that you are brought more fully into the knowledge of and obedience to His image reflected in and through you.

May the Living God give you the grace to truly trust in Him. May He forever keep you; may He guard you from the seduction of unbelief. May you forever resist the temptation to lose your heart. Walk strong in the LORD and the power of His might!

Shalom!

IF - RUDYARD KIPLING

In my presentations on "Secrets of Success" and "Do What the Successful Do, Get What the Successful Have" and, actually, in almost every presentation I deliver (even in this book), I speak of the importance and the power of reading. Part of increasing happiness is to increase your IQ. The #1 way to increase your IQ is to read!

As I have led book studies over the years, the study that I led to help educate people about money, finances, economics was called "Freedom Requires Discipline." Thus, when I walked into a retail establishment and perused the book section, Jocko Willink's book caught my attention, "Discipline Equals Freedom." I immediately picked it up wondering who had "stolen" my tagline to discover a retired Navy SEAL, Jocko Willink who's book spoke to me on almost every level.

In hindsight, I should have joined the military, but I was too rebellious, too anti-establishment, too prejudiced that only "meatheads" join the military while the "best and the brightest" study at university. Alas, Jocko Willink is one of the best, and the brightest and his intensity and excellence are admirable.

While I relish the insights Willink offered in his books, a mentee of mine introduced me to his podcast during which he discusses discipline and leadership in business, war, relationships, and everyday life. Specifically, she sent me the podcast in which he breaks down, line for line, the poem "If" by Rudyard Kipling. This poem, in and of itself, is worth reading and re-reading as it is the "The Happiness Formula" lived out. As I listened to Willink speak with his director, Echo Charles, I began to take notes of my own.

May this poem and my thoughts that follow help you begin to understand how you can incorporate more of "The Happiness Formula" into your daily walk.

If you can keep your head when all about you
Don't lose your temper. Ever. I repeat, do not lose your temper! (EQ)

Are losing theirs and blaming it on you,
Keep your cool. Control your emotions in the moment so you can own what is yours (mature adults understand the value and respect the process of being accountable) and stand firm in your truth. (EQ)

If you can trust yourself when all men doubt you,
Be confident. Trust you are capable. Know you are skilled and knowledgeable. (IQ, EQ)

But make allowance for their doubting too;
"But" (always pay attention to this word) while you have to believe in yourself, you have to be open to input that highlights your issues. (IQ) Never fear that you might be wrong or not as talented or as squared away as you think and accept your idea may not be the best. (EQ) The doubts of others might be real.
→ HUMILITY (GQ)

If you can wait and not be tired by waiting,

Patience. Life is all about patience. Patience is a virtue and one of the six fruits of the spirit (GQ) that, when practiced, (EQ) deliver love, joy, peace – happiness!

Or being lied about, don't deal in lies,
People will lie about you. (IQ) YOU tell the truth. (EQ) Period. (GQ)

Or being hated, don't give way to hating,
People will hate you, which is essentially their insecurities. (IQ) Do not let other's perceptions of you, their jealousy, their insecurity, their "hate," deter you from your path. (EQ) Simultaneously, don't feel sorry for them which is your ego. The opposite of hate is indifference – be indifferent. Yeshua says, "Shake the dust from your feet and move on."

And yet don't look too good, nor talk too wise:
Keep it real. Don't be a know-it-all or come across so virtuous no one can relate to you. Don't place yourself above people and certainly not below them. (EQ) Just be you. →
HUMILITY (GQ)

If you can dream—and not make dreams your master;
Live in reality. Daydreams do not serve a purpose. You have a shot at happiness when your life is aligned with reality. (IQ)

If you can think—and not make thoughts your aim;
Thought for the outcome of thought serves no purpose. You think to inspire action, movement, change, growth, transformation. You were not created to be The Originator of Thoughts. You exist to work in service of others. Your thoughts are designed for you to act on them! This is why you

177

must become the master of your thoughts. You control what you feed your mind. While thoughts will be fed into your mind by others and the world, outside enemies, and even "the evil one," you control what you ingest. Just because you notice a thought, does not mean you have to talk to it, get to know it, take it home and sleep with it and, god forbid, make babies with it. Notice and move on! We are told, "Take your thoughts captive." (EQ)

The Lord says to Cain, "Why is your head hung low?" Cain had spent a lot of years sleeping with greed and envy. This had born the "baby" (thought), his life would be better without his brother. The Lord continues, "Don't you know that if you do what is right, pleasing and good, the opportunity to sin (miss the mark of perfection, err in doing what is right and your duty) is always waiting at your door and then you will incur guilt which is the penalty of sin? Sin is an ever-present fixture as you go in and go out. It desires, it longs, it craves to devour you like the beast it is. But, you, Cain, I have given you all you need to master it. You are its ruler. You have dominion and reign over sin.[1] You have no reason to fear (even when it was your actions that caused these evil thoughts to enter your head, even when you opened the door to sin and let it in), for you are a child of mine. You were not given a spirit of fear (that which brings death), but you carry the DNA of The Master (which is the only way to LIFE.)[2]

---

[1] Genesis 4:7 If you do what is right, will you not be accepted? But if you do not do what is right, sin is crouching at your door; it desires to have you, but you must rule over it.

[2] Romans 8:15 The Spirit you received does not make you slaves, so that you live in fear again; rather, the Spirit you received brought about your adoption to sonship. And by him we cry, *"Abba,* Father."

In the end, it is not that we work super hard to control what goes into our head and then beat ourselves up because we keep thinking "bad" thoughts. It is an issue of knowing WHO is in control.

As for those who are paid to think (professors, preachers, teachers, consultants) your aim is still not the thoughts in and of themselves. Technically, you are NOT paid to think; you are paid to give your thoughts to another so s/he can do something productive with them. As such, thinking for the sake of thinking is never the aim. Thinking itself has a purpose. Thus, IQ (data, facts, stats, patterns, research, LEARNING) the goal is APPLICATION – EQ!

If you can meet with Triumph and Disaster
  And treat those two impostors just the same;
Neither triumph or disaster is a be all, end all. It feels like it in the moment (the glory feels glorious and the grief feels like death), but it will go away. Life will change. (IQ) Think back on the first person who broke your heart – many of us can't even remember exactly why we liked them. Think back to the first job you lost (due to layoff or firing) and you cannot even remember the names of who you worked with or exactly what was so great about the job. Now think about what it sounds like when you hear someone boast about how great they were when. To lament of past pain or boast of a past victory – both point to a person who has not grown. (EQ)

If you can bear to hear the truth you've spoken
  Twisted by knaves to make a trap for fools,
You cannot win a battle with an unscrupulous, dishonest person so don't take the bait lest you be shown a fool. Think

about it, why would you argue with someone who twists your truth? They have shown themselves to be willing to be deceptive and manipulative so be very, very careful. Sometimes you may have to defend yourself but keep your words brief. "Sin is not absent when words are many." (EQ)

Or watch the things you gave your life to, broken,
And stoop and build 'em up with worn-out tools:
Sometimes, you may have to go back to the bottom, start over and rebuild yourself because you are the worn-out tool. So, do it. (EQ)

If you can make one heap of all your winnings
And risk it on one turn of pitch-and-toss,
And lose, and start again at your beginnings
And never breathe a word about your loss;

Don't talk about the hard road you had to travel, just perform. While you have to take risks in life, should you risk it all? It may not be advisable to put it all on the line but, regardless of what troubles you have experienced, stay quiet, no need to lament or even brag. i.e.: A common exclamation I hear is either designed to impress or to convince others one is humble, "I can make millions, I just can't keep it." Regardless of the motive of the person who says this, it is not impressive when you still have nothing. It is NET RESULTS that matter! As such, it's better to learn from your mistakes and move on. (IQ/EQ)

If you can force your heart and nerve and sinew
To serve your turn long after they are gone,
When you have nothing left to give, keep giving. When your body has nothing left, no energy to go on, push forward, press on. Force your mind and your body to serve you! (EQ/GQ)

And so, hold on when there is nothing in you
Except for the Will which says to them: 'Hold on!' (GQ)

181

Time is a construct of our emotions. (IQ) When you hit mid-life, you realize one year is nothing, a blink of an eye. A 20-something, on the other hand, is ready to jump out of their skin to wait a month let alone a year. (EQ) The hidden seeds of God's plan take a long time to gestate and be revealed to us. (GQ)

If you can talk with crowds and keep your virtue,
  Or walk with Kings—nor lose the common touch,
Stay balanced. Retain your character. Stay grounded. Treat people with respect regardless of rank. (EQ)

If neither foes nor loving friends can hurt you,
It is usually those who are closest to you who can hurt you because you are more invested in them. (IQ) So you have to be careful about allowing others to "jam you up" both friend and foe. This is not about being cold-hearted, it is about recognizing we WILL get jammed up so go into any relationship knowing you WILL get hurt, expect it, and you are less likely to have your world rocked to the core of ineffectiveness. Not to mention, when someone shows you who they are (they were a friend or lover, and they mistreat you), count it a blessing because now you know who they are and you are free, you escaped, look how much you've learned, move on. (EQ)

Echo says to Jocko, "You have an over-developed control of your emotions. The normal person has open wounds, and the average person cannot immediately jump to the control of emotions."

Jocko Willink, in his classic style, recognizes it is a challenge in the midst of the pain to immediately begin to exercise control of one's emotions but, through discipline, one can. After all, what are the options? Jocko states, "You can mourn, but there is a limitation, four days, maybe. Do not wreck your life over a loss [of a person, thing, situation]. It's day three; I have two choices: dig a hole, climb in, never come out. Or, step up, make things happen, move forward. And, when you step up and move forward, soon you won't even remember that person or situation."[1]

Jocko goes on to explain that to be effective in controlling one's emotions, you need "protocol" ["The Happiness Formula"] – a set of rules and regulations you establish so you can deal with life. In expanding on the example of breaking up with a significant other, Jocko offers the following protocol:

- Day 1 after break up – Eat pizza, extra pepperoni, and drink milkshakes
- Day 2 – 8-mile run (every three months of a relationship equals 1 mile) and then a bath protocol of 5-minute ice bath, 5-minute hot bath, 4-minute ice bath, 4-minute hot bath, etc.
- Day 3 – 24-hour fast
- Day 4 – back to normal routine, get busy, get on with it

While his example is facetious, on a lot of levels it is a perfect protocol template when you have experienced a loss:

- First – Give yourself a day to hurt, lament, cry, mourn, do that which will bring you comfort (Although not at all costs

---

[1] http://jockopodcast.com/2018/08/29/140-if-by-rudyard-kipling-analyzed-not-liking-to-fight-personal-intelligence-giving-tactful-feedback/

because he specifically says "no alcohol." Hence, as long as what brings you comfort is not harmful.)

- Second – Make sure to take care of yourself physically which usually means getting physical.
- Third – Make sure to connect to God formally. Spend quality and quantity time with God.
- Fourth – Get on with your living your life!

In the end, Jocko tells us, when you see something "dragging you in the wrong direction," design a protocol which will take you in a more positive, effective direction. It is not about ignoring your emotions, it is about working through them, so they don't drag you down. (IQ)

What is even more encouraging about designing protocols to deal with painful moments in life, these same protocols can be used when you spot a yellow flag indicating "caution, danger ahead." Thus, you can implement your protocol in a pro-active fashion. It keeps you from getting into an unhealthy emotional state, a place that will drag you down.

Jocko and Echo brought up the example of Alcoholics Anonymous which designed a 12-step protocol used by hundreds of different communities to recover from addictive, compulsive, or other behavioral problems, hurts, habits, and hang-ups. The 12-step "protocol" helps one learn how to see their "triggers" (the yellow flag) such that she can take action and make decisions that will allow her to live a more effective and productive life in the moment and going forward.

While feelings are not facts they are flags of various colors: red, yellow, green, and they are last in the proper order of what is effective – Faith, Facts, Feelings. Feelings are powerful, and they can spur you on to accomplish great feats or spiral you down into hell. Thus, remember feelings are not facts, and they will change. (IQ)

If all men count with you, but none too much;

It is not about not caring what people think because we all have at least a few people for whom we care a LOT how they perceive us, we respect them and want the same. In the end, however, never consider anyone's opinion of you so much that you are distracted from your path (EQ) and, specifically, what God thinks. In the end, you will answer to the Almighty, so if you can come to peace with your walk with the Lord, people's opinions, even those who matter, will not matter "too" much. (GQ)

If you can fill the unforgiving minute
With sixty seconds' worth of distance run,

Every minute IS unforgiving because time does not stop, and you cannot get it back. Time has no mercy. Time does not consider you in its forward progress. (IQ) As such, you must care about every minute of your life if you hope to progress. (EQ) Tell me where and how you spend your time, and I will tell you what you value, who you worship, your priorities. (IQ)

Yours is the Earth and everything that's in it,

AND, if you take in every minute as precious, invaluable, irreplaceable, you WILL make forward progress because you won't waste time on that which has no value. (IQ, EQ, GQ)

And—which is more—you'll be a Man, my son!
IF you can do all of this, You WILL be a mature adult able to master the formula of life which brings happiness: IQ+EQ+GQ=HQ!

Simple, but not easy.

THF DAILY "TO-DOS"

Below are some but not all of the DAILY "to-dos" of healthy, joy-filled, successful, and FREE people who know the TRUTH that what we DO affects our happiness. Bear in mind, this list is not exhaustive but if you try to do it all, you will be exhausted! Pick a few of these daily "to dos" and incorporate them into your life over a 3-6-month period. When you have made them part of your daily lifestyle, so that you almost do not have to think about them anymore, pick a few more "to dos" and continue that pattern.

- Talk to God in the morning, at noon, and at night. Continually.
- Embrace the Truth that today is the only day you have and make decisions and take actions fully aware you will live an eternity.
- Make your bed immediately upon awakening.
- Eat breakfast.
- Spend 5-10 minutes creating your list of activities for the day while keeping your annual plan in mind so you can more effectively organize the allocation of your time.
- Drink water and more water (no sodas, alcohol, energy drinks, chemicals).
- Choose nutrient-rich foods; limit sugar intake.
- Exercise your brain: read quality fiction and mostly non-fiction at least 20 minutes per day.
- Breathe in nature: dig your toes into the grass, hug a tree, stare at the clouds, gaze at the stars. Enjoy God's creation at least 10 minutes per day.

- Exercise your body: increase your heart rate for at least 20 minutes per day four times per week minimum.
- Speak encouraging words - grace, Love and forgiveness – daily to at least one person including yourself. If you can do this with upwards of 5 people daily, get ready for the floodgates of Heaven to open!
- Squeeze someone's hand, pat someone's back, give and receive hugs up to five times a day if possible and at least once for sure!
- WORK!! Give it your all. Eight hours means eight hours of focus on the work that pays your bills!
- Give your most excellent self always! Good is the enemy of great.
- Speak with excellence. Small minds talk about people. Good minds talk about events. Great minds talk about ideas.
- Drive the speed limit. Seriously. Slow down! Let others merge.
- Choose wisely.
- Seek wisdom.
- Call upon God when you are agitated, irritable, or discontent. He will transform your mind and heart to view the world from His infinite and eternal perspective, rather than our finite and temporal myopia.
- Pause before you speak and ask yourself (1) Does it need to be said? (2) Does it need to be said right now? (3) Does it need to be said by me?
- Feelings are not facts, and they will change. Feelings are flags of various colors: red, yellow, green.
- Remember that order matters: Faith. Facts. Feelings.

- Remember Life is not about you. People are not doing it "to" you. They are just doing it.

- Don't forget you are always a good example – a good example of what TO DO or a good example of what NOT TO DO.

- Apologize in the moment if you are able and, if not, apologize within 24 hours.

- At night: Review your day for what went well, make a note to continue those behaviors, thank God for the ability to live so effectively. Review where you went astray, determine if you owe amends to anyone and commit to addressing the issue first thing the next day, ask God to help change your attitudes and actions so you can desist from that which is not effective and thank God for the beautiful pain of learning.

- Kiss your children goodnight every night, no matter how old they are, for as long as they live with you – which should not be much past their 18th birthday.

- Make love to your spouse.

- Wash your face. Brush your teeth. Thank God for blessings and hardship. Pray for others.

- Sleep at least 7-8 hours each night.

- Shabbat = Choose one 24-hour period/week to REST! Relax. Meditate. Listen. Give thanks!

ANNUAL PLANNING

Goals setting and annual planning are an imperative process to achieve whatever you seek in life. They are part of "The Happiness Formula." Because I lead workshops specifically around this process not to mention resources abound to understand its importance, below is a snapshot of how to conceptualize the process.

IQ is facts, data, stats. It's about tools and learning. It's the Goals Wheel.[1]

EQ is execution. It is about taking what one has learned and applying it to one's life.

If decades of research prove that those who have the greatest success are those who plan, one can use their IQ to learn how to plan and then use their EQ to review the plan, edit when needed, and re-apply as necessary.

You transform the muscle in your head similar to how you transform the muscles in your body. You train it. You exercise it. You work on it daily. Month after month. Year after year.

Because you ARE in control of your mind, your perception, your reality, you must take control of that from which you view your world, your circumstances, your past, your present, your future. Life is NOTHING besides how we SEE it. Life is

---

[1] You can access a copy of the one-page "Goals Wheel" I use to teach annual goal planning at https://kasandravitacca.com/applications/

ONLY what we PERCEIVE. Therefore, life is truly all about how you see yourself in this world and what is possible for you.

So how do you create a better world for you? You train your brain to see the possibilities. You do not need acid or peyote to open your mind, you need to exercise the fertile ground that is your mind, so it is ready to receive input, data, facts, stats, and all that is unknown and inexplicable. It is only AFTER you have cultivated a fertile ground, your mind is ready to receive. It is only after you have raked through and tilled up and thrown out the rocks, the weeds, and the garbage that blocks and inhibits growth. It is then that an epiphany can occur.
So how do you cultivate this fertile land of the mind?

You read. You learn. You listen to wise counsel. You apply what you have read and heard and learned. You mess up. You fail in your first and second and maybe third and fourth attempt. And you read some more. Learn new insights. Study deeper. Ask more questions. YOU SEEK! And you do not stop seeking. You never rest…nor do you worry! The outcome is not up to you anyway. Your job is the process. The work on the journey.

Too amorphous? Too ephemeral? Too academic? Too much in your head? So, what do you DO?!?!?

Take action! Make a plan! Do the next right indicated thing and then do what naturally comes after – so make the BLUEPRINT and then let's pack your tool chest with the tools that matter.

<u>Tools Matter. Actions Matter.</u>

You are a construction worker about to build the most important edifice you will ever construct – yourself! WHAT you pack in their tool chest and HOW you use these tools will allow you to create a place in which others will live and interact with you in comfort, peace, and joy – others will be happy, and you will be happy!

Blueprint
This is the overall goals list, the "Goals Wheel." This is the big picture. This is how you know which tool to use at any particular moment of the building process.

Tape measure (Faith / Spiritual)
Everything must be measured through the standards set by your God! Everything! The rest of your work will be shoddy at best and certainly will not last if you do not measure all against the standards of excellence established by your God. What can you learn, what actions can you take to increase your understanding of and relationship with your God?

Glue (Family / Communal)
If you are married, there is NO other relationship more important. None! If you are single and want to be married, how you conduct your singleness matters. Do not play married or play house before either of you have said, "I do." The family God gave you serves a purpose. You have a role in ensuring its health. You can be the glue that creates the bonds that heal. For many of us, we will create a "family" through our community. Either way, "family matters." What can you learn, what actions can you take to strengthen your familial bonds?

192

Saw (Health / Physical)

Back and forth. Back and forth. Back and forth. Yes, this is the cycle of health. Every day, day after day, week after week, year after year. Keep sawing away at your food choices and your physical activity. Intake and output are the name of the game. What can you learn, what actions can you take to become a healthier you?

Hammer (Career / Vocational)

We hammer away at our career. We pound the pavement for the right job, the right client, the right opportunity. While it might be possible to swing the hammer once and drive the nail in, it usually takes a LOT of practice, time, and patience to get it, so it feels effortless. What can you learn, what actions can you take to increase your IQ and EQ as it relates to what pays your bills? This includes "Domestic Engineers."

Nails (Education / Intellectual)

Any project uses a LOT of nails or all sorts and sizes and every time you start a new project you need more nails. So, it is with what we know. You NEVER know enough. You NEVER have all the answers. NEVER stop learning! What can you learn, what actions can you take to exercise the muscle of your brain?

Drill (Wealth / Financial)

Money is a by-product of all the effort above. It has limited and specific applications and uses. It is not the primary tool in your tool chest. It is powerful and the better you know how to handle it the more efficient you will be in all your life endeavors, but it is just a tool. What can you learn, what actions can you take to increase your financial understanding and peace?

Level (Friends / Social)

Your social network will help you stay level set because they will allow you the freedom to rest and be yourself. What can you learn, what actions can you take to deepen your social connections?

Screwdriver (Fun / Recreational)

Fun must be had! However, don't screw yourself by thinking life is all about how much "fun" you are having because, the truth is, if you do all the above well, you will already have almost all the fun you desire! What can you learn, what actions can you take to ensure you incorporate more fun into your life without sacrificing all the "must-dos" of life?

At any given time as you build your house, you may not need to use a particular tool. It's not that the tool has no value, or it won't be critical to complete another part of the job later on, but depending upon the season of life, some tools are not a priority. What is critical is the process of creating the plan, reviewing the plan, asking someone or two to hold you accountable to the plan, and revising the plan as needed because life WILL not go exactly as you had planned. The most successful people create plans with enough specificity to motivate themselves to more and with enough flexibility they can maneuver as life demands.

Traits of the Radically Successful

Given the most successful people consistently write annual plans, it is revealing to analyze the traits of these people and discover they correspond to the categories of the "Goals Wheel."

If you spend enough time reading books, research, articles, and blogs about the traits of the radically successful, you start to hear the same messages repeated. In scouring the pages of all these sources, I tracked words, phrases, and concepts to ascertain if there is a "main" list of traits worth sharing. I have deduced nine traits of the radically successful.

The traits of radically successful people are:

1. Future Oriented. (GQ)
    Optimistic; Committed; Focused; Hungry to Solve Problems; Irrationally High Level of Commitment
    o   Spiritual: It is because they have faith, the radically successful can envision a future.

2. Comfortable Being Uncomfortable. (EQ/GQ)
    Courageous Outside the Comfort Zone; Confident; Extraordinarily Creative; Rule Breakers
    o   Spiritual: It is because they have faith, the radically successful accept that while they may not always know the outcome, they know it will be abundant.

3. Organized for Change. (IQ/GQ)
   Prepared; Respond Instantly to Change; The Box is Checked for Details and Homework
   - o Familial/Communal: Because individuals are involved in all aspects of our lives, the radically successful know you cannot control what any one person does, and so they organize their life with flexibility and plan their days with contingencies.

4. Hard working. (IQ/EQ)
   Ambitious; Ferociously Driven, Determined to Work Harder Than Others
   - o Vocational: Regardless of their title, the radically successful know that to work is to serve and they engage in their daily "to-dos" with vigor.

5. Lifelong Learners. (IQ)
   Constantly Improving; Incredibly Curious; Thirsty to Learn; Never Quit Asking Questions
   - o Educational: The radically successful have great confidence in what they know and are eager to learn more especially if a new insight will correct an old way of thinking that does not serve themselves or others well.

6. Resilient and Persistent. (EQ/GQ)
   Consistent Persistence in the face of Resistance; Relentlessly Patient Overcomers
   - o Physical: The radically successful apply the correct disciplines necessary to maintain a well-functioning body, mind, and spirit knowing the majority of this

finite space and time is set up to break down their body, mind, and spirit.

7. Honorable. (IQ/EQ/GQ)
   Accountable; Responsible; Honest; Self-Reliant
   o Financial: As a created being with specific gifts, talents, and resources assigned by The Divine, the radically successful understand they are stewards in the highest calling of YHVH's image, the wealth of all that is Divine.

8. Connected to Others. (EQ)
   Provide Value; Love Playing the People Game; Elevated Communication; Supportive Network
   o Social: People matter. The radically successful know that no matter what words come out of a person's mouth, the message is always, "Accept the person I am. Listen to me."

9. Radically Present. (GQ)
   Relaxed and Balanced; Realistically Aware; Living in the Moment
   o FUN!: Life does not exist in any other time and place than right here, right now. The radically successful embrace the fullness of life's present moments with a vigor that inspires others.

While these traits correspond to the "Goals Wheel" they also align with "The Happiness Formula" and highlight all the elements of what brings happiness. Write down your plans and make yourself vulnerable such that you can discuss these plans with others. Also, know even the best-laid plans do not always go as planned. IQ reminds us, "These plans will not work out exactly as defined," EQ emboldens us, "Although the plan will ebb and morph, so will we," and, GQ gives us the hope to continue to another day, trusting and believing. "It will be better than you had even thought possible because you cannot see all that I see, you cannot know all that I know,[1] for I am your God and I love you more than myself."[2]

This final entry in the chapter "Annual Planning" is "The Happiness Formula" in full operation as it relates to MANY areas. I chose to put it in this section because it is simply an excellent example of God's plans versus are own...and how much BETTER they are than what we can possibly imagine!

Megan's story

How Do You Make God Laugh? Tell Him, "I have a plan."

"For my thoughts are not your thoughts, and your ways are not my ways," says ADONAI. As high as the sky is above the earth are my ways higher than your ways, and my thoughts than your thoughts." (Isaiah 55:8-9 CJB)

During our brief Monday call, Meagan stated she had been speaking to another financial advisor who told her the contracts she recently signed would lose her money and have negative tax implications. I informed her that we needed to

---

[1] Isaiah 55:8-9 For my thoughts are not your thoughts, neither are your ways my ways," declares the Lord. As the heavens are higher than the earth, so are my ways higher than your ways and my thoughts than your thoughts.
[2] Ephesians 2

have an in-person meeting, so I could walk her through the facts and the contractual guarantees, after which she would be assured her money was safe. She agreed to wait for my follow up email with dates and times to meet. When I sent an email the next day with meeting options over a week out, she informed me I was a liar and asked to cancel her contracts.

While I attempted to salvage the relationship, Meagan was adamant I was not trustworthy and refused to speak to my business partner or me. I was dumbfounded. A "liar"?! I was confused about how a relationship I knew was "meant to be" could end this way.

I had structured my business such that I only worked with people who I felt the Lord called me to help. I made sure potential clients understood, "While money and your financial wealth plan are why we are meeting, please know the Lord may have other plans for how I should serve you." While my ego never liked the idea that someone would choose not to do business with me, I entered the financial services business to be a servant, not a salesperson.

I genuinely liked Meagan and her husband. I could see them as "friends," which is why I also partnered with another advisor. My relationship with my clients could transform beyond the bounds of professional friendliness, and I had to ensure they never felt as if I had abandoned their wealth building strategy.

When I got gut-level honest, Megan's reaction hurt my heart. I had been rejected by someone who I sincerely wanted to help. It was a rejection of the worst kind – to be slandered by a friend with no opportunity to state my case. Yet, I had to say something because Meagan and I worked within the same community.

I wrote her a letter and explained my disappointment that she had not given me a chance to help her, because she lost a lot of money and there was no need. Specifically, I highlighted the fact that because we were professional colleagues, she would be out of line to disparage me especially without proof of any wrongdoing on my part. She never acknowledged my letter in writing or in person, and we had multiple professional interactions after the incident. While we were both cordial, I always wondered what exactly happened that she lost faith in me as a professional and, more importantly, as a woman of integrity. She was more than cordial when we were together; she was warm and friendly. I was confused.

Three years later, I found myself sitting next to Meagan at a professional association's annual conference and I had to address the elephant in the room, "Meagan, would you mind speaking to me about what happened all those years ago? We are leaders within this association, and I would like to bring some closure to a situation I never fully understood." I barely finished my sentence when Meagan immediately began to apologize and explain the personal "chaos" that had become her life during that time. She made it clear she knew I was an honorable woman and that I had not lied. She confessed she was under so much pressure and so confused in her personal life, "I just lost it for a little while."

We ended our time together in an embrace agreeing to let bygones be bygones.

Three more years passed and I heard the Lord tell me to talk to Meagan about Him. I was very nervous to ask Meagan my initial question. We had been discussing business, and I flipped the script:

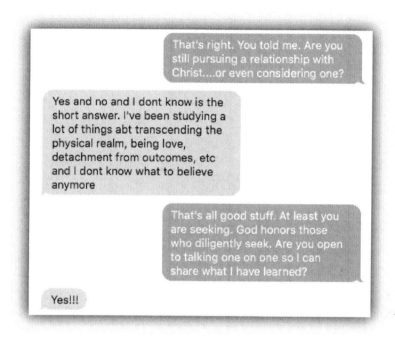

Megan and I met at a local deli and spent a few hours talking. I shared how I came to know Christ and, in the process, answered a lot of her questions. About three hours into our conversation, I found myself saying words I had no control over, "Do you think you are ready to make a decision for Christ?" Meagan sat up straighter and eagerly replied, "Yes!" At which point, I went into crisis prayer mode as I had no idea what to do next – but God!

I grabbed Meagan's hands in that crowded deli and told her I would pray, and at some point, she should repeat after me. All the noise of the lunchtime diners faded away, and the air stood still as I thanked God for Meagan's life and her desire to claim her inheritance as His daughter and my sister. I eventually asked Meagan to repeat after me and ask God to accept her as she accepts Him as her Lord and Savior. She confessed her need for Him and thanked Him for His sacrifice on the Cross so she would not have to endure the full consequence of her sin and missing the mark of His perfection.

I closed out the prayer thanking God that Meagan is a new creation, fully redeemed, fully transformed, holy, righteous, blameless and pure, perfectly provided for, perfectly secure, as He is now in charge of her life. Meagan began to cry. She knew she had become a Daughter of the God of Most High, and so did I.

A relationship that began in 2012 with a business agreement that ended poorly, six years later transformed into what God had in mind all along – He wanted His daughter to come back home!

CONFESSION – In 2012, when I told Meagan that "money" is my excuse to have conversations with people while I figure out what God has planned for me as His servant, I was not fully aware what I was saying. So, if you ask me today, "What do you do?" I might answer, "I am a servant of God cleverly disguised as a Financial Advisor, Speaker, and Author."

HOW THF APPLIES TO HEALTH

Everything I put on looked horrible on me. I couldn't get dressed for work because everything showed my body and if it covered my body up enough, I looked sloppy because it was obvious I was trying to cover up. I was fat!

But I wasn't fat. I was sick. I had body dysmorphia. I was sick and tired of looking in the mirror and seeing flaws and imperfections and "a little too much" here and a "not flat enough" part there. Somewhere in the back of my mind, I had a mustard seed of faith that maybe I was not as big and unattractive as I saw in the mirror but, alas, I could not tell. I could only see flaws, imperfection, "fat." I felt this way despite the data of how tall I was (5'6") related to my weight (138-143 lbs) which was considered normal. I felt this way despite many compliments I had received about my appearance. What I saw was a "huge" woman. And I was sick of my mental distortion, my obsession.

In 2007, I applied the process of "The Happiness Formula."

- IQ: All the facts from the numbers to the reports of others indicate I am a healthy, not-fat woman. Is there anything more I can do or learn to increase my understanding of how to be healthy and fit? Can I change my diet even more? Can I change my exercise routine?
- EQ: While the data tells me I am not fat and while I am doing everything in my human power to effect changes, I still feel fat BUT, feelings are not facts. I choose to believe

what the data reveals. I choose to let the process of increased awareness of and commitment to better choices in my diet and exercise routine run their course. I will be patient as my body and mind transform which is the only possible result as I stick to the plan.

- GQ: Forgive me Lord for my obsessive focus on my body such that it distracts me from productive and positive activities. You know I don't want to think these thoughts and, yet, You have not taken them away. I trust there is a reason for me to be blind to my physique as well as for why I place it so high on my list of values that it robs me of joy. I know either I will get comfortable being uncomfortable in my body or You will completely remove my obsession, and I will see with clarity.

On my wedding day, October 27, 2013, I weighed 143 lbs. My husband asserts I was anorexic. At 5'6" with a medium frame, I was not remotely underweight. My body had always been healthy and strong, and it was the weight I had been used to since my college days in the late 80s/early 90s.

Fast forward to 2018, and the scale consistently rests at 155 lbs. While it might teeter upwards to 158 lbs. or even drop to 152 lbs., my new "normal" for the past couple of years seems to be the mid-150s. I ran a half marathon in May 2016, and after six months of training, the scale never dropped below 152 lbs.

For a woman who has suffered body-dysmorphia her whole life, getting comfortable with a weight that by all body mass indices places me in the "overweight" category intrigues me. Even a recent doctor visit confirmed that I am technically overweight and need to lose at least 5lbs and 10-15 lbs. would be more "normal."

Seriously?! I have to do more than the five days of hot yoga, Pilates, and core workouts I already do weekly? I have to do more than the relatively simple, clean meals that my family consistently critiques as "boring" and "healthy"? I have to cut out the delicious baked goods that I used to make weekly but have cut back to once a month?! Sure, I can do more but, seriously, I don't want to!

I am close to 50 years old, and for the first time in my life, I do not abhor my body. I do not feel super sexy, and I would rather not be naked but, alas, I am strong and capable and full of energy and, at the base, I do not feel "ugly." Do I seriously need to do more?

In the summer of 2009, I prayed to God to remove the insanity of my body image problems. I finally incorporated GQ into this specific area of my life equation and began to experience some freedom. For 18 months, I had worked with a personal trainer, wrote down every morsel I consumed, and wore a body device 24/7 that measured my actual caloric expenditure. This was before it dawned on me to ask God (rather plead with YHVH) to remove the obsession. It was then that I admitted I was powerless over the feeling of being "fat, flawed, and ugly," and I began to experience some relief.

For almost a decade, I did my part to get "happy" with my body. I became a veritable expert in health as I engaged my IQ to learn all I could about nutrition and exercise. My EQ rose as I applied what I was learning, and I finally permitted myself to tell others of my struggle. I followed the 12-steps of recovery to find release and came to accept body-dysmorphia as a chemical misfire in my brain or the thorn in my side that keeps me dependent on a Higher Power or something beyond my ultimate control. But I had a mustard seed of "want" to be HAPPY with my body.

It is now 2018. For almost 40 years, I have only seen my flaws. But now I can finally see I am a healthy middle-aged woman. While I am not ready to walk the runway, I can finally see myself as attractive. I am finally at peace, full of joy, and free of an addiction which plagued me almost all my life. I am finally relieved of the burden of body-dysmorphia.

Only now I am officially, technically, overweight. The irony is downright humorous.

So, will I do anything different? Now that I have the facts (IQ), will I change my behaviors (EQ)?

Absolutely not! My IQ knows how to read the numbers on the scale as well as the plethora of research that calls into question the BMI standards. More importantly, my EQ has risen enough that I know what I am willing to do and not do about my diet and exercise. Finally, I am most relieved and grateful that there is a God in Heaven who can and will restore us to sanity. (HQ)

So, what does all this mean for you? I am going to say that which is not popular but, alas, people harm themselves by their poor eating and exercise habits. My heart breaks for people when they get diseases and cancers and need knee and hip replacements and have heart attacks, and life is otherwise less than joy-filled physically. Simultaneously the truth is your body reacts to the fuel you put into it throughout ALL your life. If you do not pay attention to ALL food and drink intake and exercise regularly, of course, your body will break down in all sorts of painful and ugly and even deadly ways.

Because I am not a fitness professional or a nutritionist and this is not a book about those topics, I will again offer a list of ideas, what I do, to stay healthy and HAPPY!

- Sleep 7-8 hours each night.
- Rise early, before sunrise is best.
- Meditate and pray and sit still each day for about 10 minutes ideally outside in the sun, the grass, in nature or even just look at God's creation.
- Exercise daily for at least 20 minutes at least 4x/week. Consider yoga, Pilates, barre – low impact exercise.
- Take supplements and probiotics as there is no way you get enough nutrition based on your diet.
- Drink water, lots and lots and lots of water!
- No sodas or alcohol. If you insist on alcohol, limit to no more than a glass a day. That's it!
- Buy food you have to make from "scratch."
- Avoid processed foods and NO fast food!
- Do NOT fry food.
- Limit sugar intake. If you must eat dessert, split it with someone or have two bites: the first bite to see if it tastes good, the second bite because it does!
- Limit breads dramatically, including chips, tortillas, pasta, naan, and rice.

- Eat lots of veggies.

Remember, the God-given purpose of food is FUEL. It is not for pleasure. Does it taste good? Yes. Is it enjoyable and part of how we connect with people? Yes. Is it one of the best ways to show love – cook someone a meal, buy a box of chocolates, treat someone to ice cream? Yes! But still, food is for fuel. If you seek "lesser gods" in food via the wrong motive, you will "miss the mark" of God's perfection for food's value in your life. If you seek food for more than its purpose, you will "sin" with food and experience over-indulgence or even under-indulgence, both do not give your body the fuel it needs.

HOW THF APPLIES TO WEALTH

I opened my eyes, but it didn't matter because the room was so dark I could not see my hand in front of me. It was cold, and the air was wet, strange noises surrounded me, and it smelled bad, like something had died. Not to mention the floor felt like it was moving. Where the hell was I? I felt the walls and found I was in a narrow passageway. I had no idea what direction to walk to get out! I began screaming. "Hello! Can anyone hear me? Help! Where am I? Someone? Anyone? Please?" I fell to the ground, sobbing as catastrophic thoughts raced through my mind. I was so tired. In fact, I was exhausted. I just wanted to lie down and fall asleep and never wake up. So I tried. I laid down on the wet, stinky floor, and swatted at insects as I cried, hoping for the end.

Then I remembered my son depends on me, I have friends, I have a life I want to keep living. In desperation, I applied what I now consider to be "The Happiness Formula."

- IQ: I knew I didn't know where I was, but I need to get out.
- EQ: I was terrified and exhausted, but I wanted to live, so I chose a direction and started to walk.
- GQ: I trusted that God was with me and that if I was meant to perish here, so be it. But I chose to believe He would lead me out.

I walked miles before I glimpsed light. I started to run toward it but fell and scraped my knees and hands. The light grew stronger and I began to hear the faint voices of my mother, my sister, my friends. Tears of hope streamed down my face and I screamed for help. Some of my strength returned and I raced toward the doorway.

When I broke free of the dark tunnel, my family and loved ones threw their arms around me, "We could hear you scream, Kasandra, but we couldn't do anything for you. We knew you were in pain, but we could not get through the door to help you. We've been here the whole time listening to your screams. We could even hear you stumble and fall and knew you were hurt, but we could not get through."

It was 2008, and I had finally crawled my way out of the pit. I was never in a physical tunnel, but the prior ten years were a tunnel experience, as I tried to be the "god" of my own life. Now I was unemployed with $14,000 in debt left by my ex-husband who I kicked out after his multiple affairs. I was on the verge of sending my son to live with his father while I, a double-degreed graduate from Stanford, moved to a homeless shelter.

- IQ: Is there enough money to get through this month? Yes. Am I healthy enough to start making calls to get a job? Absolutely. Am I willing to take any job as long as it is legal and ethical? Yes.
- EQ: Do I feel like a big failure? Yes. Am I a failure? No. Will this current situation last forever? No. Has my ego been massively deflated? Hell yes. Did it need to be? Probably.

210

- GQ: Has God always provided? Yes. Has He ever let me be homeless and hungry? No. Do I think God is trying to show me that His provision and protection is better than my own? Yes.

And so, the financial rebuilding began. In 2008, I entered the world of financial services. I started as a recruiter for an independent financial services practice while I learned the business. By 2010, I went 100% commission as an independent representative of insurance contracts while partnering with others in the firm who managed investments. I made over six figures that year and continued to increase my business by about 40% every year after that until I went part-time in 2014.

As part of my business approach, I simply taught people what I did in my life. Please note, rebuilding myself financially such that I not only had more money but more peace, joy, freedom – happiness – around my money, did not take too long. Within five years, I was in a better financial position than I had ever been in and within ten years, I entered the coveted ranks of the 1%. Bottom line, "The Happiness Formula" works when you work it.

Speaking to individuals about their money via the assets of insurance and investments is one of my businesses. I present webinars and live presentations about financial education. What follows is a very high-level list that will require more dialogue to understand and incorporate into your life. However, these truths are some of what is fundamental to everything I teach about money.

1. Save: 20% of everything you make. This should go towards your option years (aka: retirement)
2. Pay bills – take care of responsibilities to yourself and others. Charity is a bill.
3. Pay down debt via a "debt laddering" system, so you do not compromise simultaneous savings
4. Spend is last in the proper order of #Save20PayBillsThenSpend. Freedom, frivolity, and pleasure is earned! If nothing is left over, wait, be patient, one day in the not too distant future, you will have extra.
5. Do not spend your time enamored by things you cannot afford. Spend your time focusing on doing what it takes to get to the next level.
6. "Smart" financing incurs an interest rate of about 5% or less because cash is king. Big ticket items (cars, houses) usually should be financed with no rush to pay down faster. If you have extra, save in your option years plan.
7. Keep 2-3 months of living expenses in your checking/savings account.
8. Keep 6-12 months living expenses in your whole life insurance cash value.
9. Invest only up to the match in company 401K.
10. Start a managed money account with at least $10K and keep adding.
11. Investments in real estate, gold, private businesses, bitcoins are all "part time" jobs. YOU must be prepared to manage the process and deal with the loss. The greater the risk, the greater the probability of loss (not the greater the reward).
12. College savings is an expense, so it should be built up in whole life insurance cash value (where you won't lose the compound interest growth), as opposed to an investment

asset (which should not be called an investment as the intent was a "delayed expense" and not future growth).

13. For W2 earners: A networking marketing business is the easiest and least expensive way to become a business owner, which is one of the main ways to mitigate taxes, even if you never work it full time.

Some of what is listed in these bullets may be new or confusing and may even make you feel less happy. Let your feelings be a call to action that you might need to learn more. I know a good team of financial professionals with whom you can seek this knowledge!

Finally, do not forget wisdom from one of the more oft-quoted leaders in history, Winston Churchill, "In finance, everything that is agreeable is unsound, and everything that is sound is disagreeable."

HOW THF APPLIES TO RELATIONSHIPS (MARRIAGE)

I was a bit numb as I sat on the couch wondering what the hell I had just done again. I was in my first year of another marriage and it was not going so well. My "magical magnifying mind" (aka: "The Horriblizer") already had me 10 years older than the present moment, without a job, penniless because he drained all our accounts as he and his younger girlfriend with whom he cheated on me traveled the world. I was sick to my stomach as these horror films played through my head. The fear was so palpable that I literally could not move. Then I started the process I now call "The Happiness Formula."

- IQ: Am I married to a faithful man? Do I have a career that I can scale up and down anytime I choose for as long as I want? Am I healthy and capable and have I taken care of myself for 25+ years?
- EQ: What are you afraid of? What past hurts from other relationships are you projecting into your current reality? What does the event which caused the nightmare thoughts tell you about your ego? Is your own selfishness driving the fear?
- GQ: Who do you ultimately trust? Hasn't God always provided food, shelter, clothing, and more? Even during your darkest times, didn't He pull you through?

After a few minutes of walking myself through "The Formula," I no longer felt terrified. I knew the chemicals from my over emotionalism needed to work themselves out of my system. To come off an emotional hangover is not always as bad as an alcohol and drug-induced one, but I still had to get into positive action quickly to speed up the "sobriety" process.

I got off the couch and did the next right indicated thing as defined by the to-do list I had for the day, and I was happy!

Below are two lists for how to have a happy marriage. The first is a list I created as part of a workshop on "How to Have a Successful Marriage" and the second is from a presentation given by Family Life, a non-profit with the mission to effectively develop godly marriages and families who change the world one home at a time. The good news is, the lists have a lot of overlap.

How to Have a Phenomenally Successful Marriage:

1. Get married for the right reason, to honor God with your covenantal oneness. Marriage is not about your happiness, but about your holiness! If you are not prepared to "die to self" to honor the other while always placing God first, you are not ready. We make a decision to be the type of person who honors this type of commitment.

2. Put the marriage before the kids! Kids leave at 18 and you will want to make sure you had focused on each other more than the kids. Do not forget, you are "one" in everything you do when it comes to the kids so make sure you discuss all the aspects of child-rearing. You won't agree on everything but

215

keep talking until you come to a respectful decision that honors you both.

3. Combine all your income, share all your passwords, and keep NO secrets! That's pretty much it. No caveats. No alternatives. No "just in case" bank accounts. If you feel the need to "protect yourself," don't get married. This includes pre-nuptial agreements. Leave that to the Hollywood crowd who play a game similar to "Fantasy Football" for who will marry who and when will they get divorced.

4. Talk to each other every day for at least 60 minutes about life, dreams, hopes, fears, joys, your union, God! If you cannot find the time to focus on each other daily, your marriage will suffer. Period. If you miss a day here or there, that is understandable, but the path to marital peace is to make each other a priority.

5. Retain your own uniqueness by enjoying separate hobbies and friends and adventures that you can share via storytelling. Do not demand the details of every minute and every word that was said when they hung out with their buddies. Respect your spouse's discernment about what is shared and not shared. Their friends will trust and respect you more when they know they can speak to your spouse without it automatically being downloaded to you. Now re-read #3 about secrets.

6. Enjoy activities together that are about the two of you. Vacations for just the two of you and weekend getaways are ideal. Be creative with your budget. A date night once a month is ideal. A weekend getaway once a quarter is ideal. Be smart with your finances and make sure the focus is about each other

and time away and not about how grand you can make the adventure each time. Be judicious about posting your adventures so that you do not distract from your time together.

7. Have an annual plan and budget! Review at least monthly. Stick to it and alter only after much discussion. You will absolutely need a wealth coach. Not just a financial advisor, someone committed to the health of your marriage. I might know someone who can help. (www.kasandravitacca.com)

8. Wives: make love to your husband as much as he wants. Husbands: don't expect your wife to have sex with you every day. Sexual relations are a gift from God to increase intimacy. Period. The purpose of sex is intimacy much like the purpose of food is fuel. If you seek satisfaction and satiation above and beyond the original purpose, you will NOT experience the abundant joy that is possible. But if you want to increase the success of your marriage, stay sexually active regardless of how you feel!

9. Stay in shape! Be healthy! Aging is expected, but excessive weight and sickness due to your inattention to your body's proper nutritional and exercise needs are not acceptable. The same applies to depression and emotional disorders. There is an opioid epidemic in our country so I do NOT advise pills for every malady. On the other hand, if you truly need mood-altering medication, take it!

10. Take turns praying for and with each other every night before going to bed. Or before making love! I repeat, take turns praying for each other every night. Hold hands, pray, give

thanks to God for each other, make your requests known to the Lord and each other. Kiss!

"5 Ways to Keep Fire Burning in Marriage"[1]

1. Make sure the marriage is built upon foundation of commitment to Christ and covenant to one another.

   - Pray with your spouse every day (only 3% pray daily w/spouse)

   "These words I speak to you are not incidental additions to your life, homeowner improvements to your standard of living. They are foundational words, words to build a life on. If you work these words into your life, you are like a smart carpenter who built his house on solid rock. Rain poured down, the river flooded, a tornado hit—but nothing moved that house. It was fixed to the rock. "But if you just use my words in Bible studies and don't work them into your life, you are like a stupid carpenter who built his house on the sandy beach. When a storm rolled in and the waves came up, it collapsed like a house of cards." (Matthew 7:24-27 The Message)

2. Quench fatal attractions that cause destructive fires
   - Take preventive measures, be proactive in protecting marriage.
   - Make sure you have consistent date nights.
   - Do not build your marriage around the kids.

---

[1] Family Life hosts an annual marriage cruise "Love Like You Mean It." In 2018 my husband and I went on the cruise and these are my brief notes from the session.

- Quench the emotional affairs!

  Can a man scoop fire into his lap without his clothes being burned?
  Can a man walk on hot coals without his feet being scorched?
  (Proverbs 6:27-28 NIV)

3. Husbands: Learn to understand your wife
   - What a women's needs in reverse order:
     - o   5-family commitment
     - o   4-security
     - o   3-honesty/openness
     - o   2-conversation
     - o   1-affection (nonsexual)
   - Listen intentionally to your wife.
   - Three questions to ask your wife:
     - o   1 - What is one of your favorite romantic moments in our marriage and why?
     - o   2 - What are the top three needs you have right now?
     - o   3 - What is one thing you want us to do on our next outing? What is the desire of your heart?

4. Wives: Spark a flame by being a magnet to your husband

- Be a student of your husband at all times.
- Respect your husband for who he is.
- Believe in your husband.
- Receive your husband.
- Three questions to ask your husband:
  - o 1 - How can I do a better job of encouraging you as a leader?
  - o 2 - Would you rather be loved or respected?
  - o 3 - When have you felt most respected by me?

5. Create a relational adventure full or romance, intrigue, and surprise.

FINAL THOUGHTS

The door was open and the fresh breeze of the autumn air filled the kindergarten classroom. We sat in two semi-circles just behind the masking tape which defined our space as the teacher explained we would elect class officers. "I want to be the president," was the first thought that entered my head without any other feelings besides I knew I was a leader. The teacher asked us to discuss who would like to serve in what role. I was quickly told by several boys and girls that a girl is not a president, she is a secretary. It was the early 70s and I was only five years old. I had no life experience to counter their assertions, so I accepted the role of secretary. I told myself that at least I was still a class leader. But I was not happy with what seemed like a decision based in, at best, faulty logic.

And so, my journey along the feminist trail began!

When Jimmy Carter was elected President in 1976, I identified with his daughter Amy as she was a "girl in the White House" and I knew I belonged there too. I had hope! By high school, I was the class president all four years. I could have tried out for cheerleader, but I wanted to have people cheering for me rather than be on the sidelines cheering for others.

I ran for Associated Student Body President my junior year. I was told the ASB Counselor encouraged a male friend to run because, "You can't let a girl win." My stomach turned, but I told my friend to run given he was honest enough to tell me this. When he won, I resolved that thereafter I would be an advocate for gender equality. I even wrote about this experience on my college essay. I am convinced it is what earned me a full ride to Stanford University.

Stanford was a bastion of rebellion against the status quo. They taught us how to think, how to research, and how to debate. Our goal was to break down the social, political, economic and emotional barriers that allow people to stay in their self-created bubbles of comfort, security, bias, and exclusion. I happily championed the cause of the disenfranchised and actively fought against the established group-think of what I saw as a male-dominated society. This was followed by activism against a white-dominated society.

I was not raised to see myself as part of the white community only. My mother was part Hunkpapa Lakota Sioux. She grew up in a segregated society and had to fight people who called her the "n-word" and other racial epithets because they were not sure what she was. After all, what does an Indian look like? She was dark and her parents who adopted her were black so, whatever she was, she was not accepted by the dominant white culture. Hence, I too identified with the historically disenfranchised, the underdog.

I also grew up in a "broken" home with no father present. The woman across the street was a single mom raising three kids and my babysitter also came from a single-mom household, so it was normal to not see a lot of dads. We came from a lower middle class, blue-collar neighborhood. The kids I grew up with tried cigarettes, alcohol, and marijuana much too young. Most of us were having sex by middle school and high school for sure. But I lived another reality. In high school, I was the class president, yearbook editor, varsity volleyball and softball starter, Girls State Representative, and voted "Most Likely to Succeed." I was accepted at USC, Yale, and Stanford where I received the full-ride scholarship.

At Stanford, however, the stakes were higher. Now I was among some of the nation's most intelligent and most privileged. Many were world-traveled and multi-lingual. I had been only to Mexico as an exchange student. Many students came from private schools which offered all AP classes. My high school offered only two AP classes. I had a huge "poor kid" chip on my shoulder, which caused me to doubt whether I had what it took to be among the nation's "elite." I felt disadvantaged, so I did what I had always done, study hard and get straight 'A's because, after all, success is all about grades, correct? Success is all about who graduates top of the class, isn't it?

When I started my sophomore year at Stanford, I switched my major from International Relations with a Russian/Soviet emphasis and decided the best way to change the world and help people be better versions of themselves so war and pain and suffering end, is to teach! Furthermore, the wall had come down in Berlin and the Cold War was over. I was no longer "needed" to help end world tension and stop a possible WWIII, which is what I set out to do when I entered college.

I continued to work hard and the straight 'A's paid off. I got another full-ride to study for a Master's at Stanford which culminated in an offer to go to Oxford and study for my PhD. But by then I was ready to take a break from college. College was not the "time of my life." I was focused on getting straight 'A's and doing whatever it took to get a good job after school.

After I earned my Masters, I went to work in a high school teaching history and coaching volleyball.

Alas, high school teachers do not make enough money for the amount of emotional garbage they must contend with. Some parents expect teachers, who are dealing with 150-200 students a day, to make "special" concessions for their child. The early 90s saw an increase in "individualized" curriculums due to the need to meet the "emotional needs of a student" (lest we jeopardize their self-esteem). I found I was not emotionally mature enough to stay focused on teaching. I made the transition into adult education and began to work in adult professional settings. From the mid-90s to around 2006, I was in a very dark place. I would often think to myself, "I have so much of what society calls 'success' or reasons for happiness and, yet, I am not happy!" I was lost and miserable most of the time. I got fired in 2005 and lost all that I valued, work, career, performance, my identity.

That propelled me to seek help and a God, and life has only gotten better since!

Throughout all this time, I have remained in my calling, to teach, to share knowledge, to encourage others to be a better version of themselves. This is my mission regardless of my job title, industry, or what service I provide. I am a teacher because I have always known that seeking knowledge and getting educated IS the key to personal improvement for myself and others. At this point, my mid-life, my goal is to help others achieve their happy.

"The Happiness Formula" is for those who are ready to simply BE. People are so eager to be unique, to express their individuality, to be different. I believe the best way to do that is to praise your God with a passion and a HAPPINESS that blows people's minds! If you have found the true God, the One Who Saves, you will experience outrageous, abundant happiness in a way that people will ask you, "What are you doing? Who are you that you can be this happy?"

To be in the world but not of the world is truly supernatural. It is inexplicable and even unbelievable. Therefore, if you want to be different, be unbelievable! Relish the moments when people question your overflow of love, peace, joy, and abundance. Still acknowledge your hurts and frustrations—and theirs. Acknowledge that God will use us for the purposes of others and it won't always feel good. If you are a parent, you may have come to accept this because you love your child beyond yourself. Can you imagine how our Good Parent feels about you—and about ALL of His children? While we are everything to Him, it is not all about us.

God created each of us with unique talents and skills and even habits and hang-ups for a reason, for a purpose. The purpose is to be of maximum service to Him and others. Don't lose sight of your purpose.

When you know the purpose of things, you get more enjoyment from them. For example, the purpose of food, even though it tastes good, is to fuel your body. The purpose of lovemaking, even though it feels good, is to fuel your marriage intimacy. If you seek the feeling over the purpose, these acts can become distorted and unsatisfying.

Rewire your brain by doing something different. Use your left hand. Drive the speed limit all the time. Stop doing something for at least three months so you can assess how it feels to go without "x". Start doing something every day for 90 days and analyze what you have learned about yourself. Read a Proverb a day. Pray for your enemies by asking God to give them triple-fold what you want for yourself. He already knows you don't "mean" it, you don't want them to prosper, that you don't "feel" like praying for them. Do it anyway. You have to be intentional about anything and everything in life.

This time and space as we know it is essentially a "holding pattern." It's the training ground. This life is not a period; it is a comma. And it is possible for this timeframe of our eternal Life to be full of love, joy, peace, and outrageous happiness, as you exercise patience, kindness, goodness, faithfulness, humility, self-control. Nothing in the Torah, the Law, stands against such things.

Nobody drinks coffee the first time and thinks, "That is delicious!" We drink for the effect. Therefore, bring everything to the Light and be honest about what you really think and feel about all of it. No longer delude yourself by saying, "This time will be different." Use your IQ to see the patterns and your EQ to accept the reality of the patterns so you choose different behaviors. Without GQ, you cannot sustain the peace, joy, freedom – happiness – that is the result of all the work you have just put in to acquire more IQ and EQ. "To thine own self be true."

Sit in your current space and time and just be. Even when we binge watch TV shows, we have decided to take the action of inaction and escape. We will fill the space and time of our finite stay in this temporal place with something. So, choose well and do not forget that sometimes that which we deem as "good" may not be. It may be from "Tree of Good and Evil."

Forget "balance." Balance does not equal excellence. Balance means I focus on everything equally, so I am good at nothing. Focus equals excellence. Focus means you have chosen what matters most right now. Other things will be out of focus until you refocus your gaze. Balance is essentially "multitasking" and multitasking is proven to be least effective and more stress-inducing. Focus allows for excellence and calm. You cannot win against someone who will outwork you; who is focused. You cannot have your highest level of happiness without focus.

The #1 thing we can focus on in this moment, is the moment. You can be so present that you experience the fullness of every moment. So many people are stuck in the past or afraid of the future. They are simply not present. They are formulating what they are going to say next, what you think about their outfit, if they have a piece of spinach in their teeth, or if that cute person across the way is single.

Life will go by in the blink of an eye if you are not present. You will wonder, "Where did all the time go?" When you focus on the present and slow down your mind, you will realize how much time you have. Being intentional about your time gives you more. Not planning your time will cause you to run out of it.

When you have incorporated "The Happiness Formula" into your life day after day, month after month, year after year, it has been my experience, you will know you have chosen well. You will know you have chosen LIFE. You will be happy!

"So where are all the happy people?" This was the question another mentee asked me. "Where do they meet up? Where do they hangout?" to which I responded:

> "Alas, a truly happy person is not a groupie. They will be part of groups, they may even have a leadership role in groups and champion the group cause, but they <u>choose</u> to participate in a group, not out of need, but to be of service. They always walk solo, but never alone. So, if you are looking for 'your people,' – the happy ones – you will find them randomly, across all groups, ages and stages, backgrounds and ethnicities, social status and vocations. You will find them like the island of misfit toys, and they will drift in and out of your life for reasons and seasons and very, very few, for a lifetime. Very few.

I am having a lot of fun on the island of misfit kids. I pray I meet you there!

Shalom!

AFTERWORD

I hope this book has given you many ways to include "The Happiness Formula" in your life. I love sharing and I want to stay connected with all the media available. I provide online 1-on-1 coaching, and I would be delighted to speak to your organization, company, social club. Let me know how I can add value and benefit to your world.

To this end, make sure you are on my mailing list by visiting www.kasandravitacca.com and inputting your contact information. At my site you can sign up for webinars that dive a bit deeper into some of the topics presented in this book. If you are in a position to hire speakers, invite me into your professional organizations and social clubs. I speak on all things leadership, wealth, and happiness so let me know how I can customize my research to meet your needs.

Finally, tell me how to pray for you. My email is on my website. If I do not respond within 48 hours, please send me another message as sometimes my inbox gets so full, I miss messages and I certainly do not want to miss yours.

"May God bless you and protect you; the Lord make His face shine upon you and be gracious to you; the Lord lift up His countenance upon you and give you peace." (Numbers 6:24-26)

May the God of hope fill you with all joy and peace as you trust in him, so that you may overflow with hope by the power of the Holy Spirit. (Romans 15:13)

May the Lord be pleased to help you serve Him in truth. [1 Peter 2:9]

Shalom!

MY PRAYER STAPLES

The Serenity Prayer

God, grant me the serenity to accept the things I cannot
change,
the courage to change the things I can,
and the wisdom to know the difference.
Living one day at a time,
enjoying one moment at a time;
accepting hardship as a pathway to peace;
taking, as Jesus did, this sinful world as it is, not as I would
have it;
trusting that You will make all things right if I surrender to
your will;
so that I may be reasonably happy in this life,
and supremely happy with You forever in the next.
Amen

Prayer of St. Francis

Lord make me an instrument of your peace
Where there is hatred,let me sow love
Where there is injury, pardon
Where there is doubt, faith
Where there is despair, hope
Where there is darkness, light
And where there is sadness, joy
O divine master grant that I may
not so much seek to be consoled as to console
to be understood as to understand
To be loved as to love
For it is in giving that we receive
it is in pardoning that we are pardoned
And it's in dying that we are born to eternal life
Amen

Thomas Merton – *Thoughts in Solitude*

My Lord God,
I have no idea where I am going.
I do not see the road ahead of me.
I cannot know for certain where it will end.
Nor do I really know myself, and the fact that I think that I
am following your will does not mean that I am actually
doing so.
But I believe that the desire to please you does in fact please
you.
And I hope I have that desire in all that I am doing.
I hope that I will never do anything apart from that desire.
And I know that if I do this, you will lead me by the right
road though I may know nothing about it.
Therefore, I will trust you always though I may seem to be
lost and in the shadow of death.
I will not fear, for you are ever with me, and you will never
leave me to face my perils alone.
Amen

TRUISMS TOO GOOD NOT TO SHARE

I believe God gives us messages all day long if we will only listen. I have compiled this list of concepts from things I have read and heard. I hope they increase your knowledge, insight, and wisdom as they encourage you to THINK (IQ), ACT (EQ) and ALIGN (GQ) your life such that HAPPINESS is the only possible result!

- Spirituality is something you do, not something you think.
- Listen for the similarities, not the differences.
- Great minds discuss ideas; average minds discuss events; small minds discuss people.
- For many, high school never ends. Just because people get older, does not mean they get wiser.
- Anytime you feel agitated, irritable or discontent, there is something amiss within you!
- Feelings are not facts, and they will change. Feelings are flags of various colors: red, yellow, green.
- Remember that order matters: Faith. Facts. Feelings.
- Life is not about you.
- Don't forget you are always a good example either of what to do, or what not to do.
- I am not where I want to be, but I am far away from where I was.
- I still have wreckage, but I don't have to make it worse.

- I found the floor of my life. Now I know what is okay and not okay.
- I had to rebuild who I was. Now I have the opportunity to be who I always wanted to be.
- Think in the third person. Be your most interesting case study.
- I am the genesis of my misery.
- We cannot differentiate between the truth and the false.
- I go on emotional dry benders. I cannot afford the luxury of over-emotionalism.
- "They" are not my problem. My problem is how I respond to them.
- My ability to be okay with life on life's terms is in direct proportion to how I feel about myself.
- My self-importance is based on my low self-esteem.
- I may not be much, but I am all I think about.
- If I get used to being uncomfortable, I don't want to do what makes me comfortable.
- Where are my feet? Stay focused on my present moment and space.
- My character defects were how I survived. They are a way of life
- My spiritual relationship is reliance, not dependence. It's a choice.
- Repetition strengthens and confirms.
- Don't take yourself so seriously.
- At some point, you have to transition from a person-doing to a person-being.
- We cease fighting all people and all things--because we have to!

- I get grumpy when I am afraid that I won't get what I need. But in God I already have everything.
- God loves me right now just as I am.
- It's not how I was brought up; it's how I ended up that counts.
- When I find myself overworking, it may mean I am not allowing God to take charge.
- Put your thoughts into words and analyze them.
- Life happens to us, but we can always make better decisions.
- I can explain it to you, but I can't understand it for you.
- Defiance = Rationalizing what I don't need.
- Look for the miracles in every day.
- If you can't figure out the math problem, what makes you think you can figure out God?
- I do NOT need to know how it is going to turn out.
- God is not about me being in control. God is about me letting go of the need for control.
- The more I hang out in the playground of faith, the more I realize it is designed for my pleasure.
- If God wants me to have something, He will make it available to me.
- God doesn't move; I move. He honors those who seek. Faith is an action.
- I don't have to know why!
- It is safe to feel.
- It might be fun at the top of the mountain, but the growth occurs in the valley.
- I don't have to understand something completely before I can accept it.

- To trust God with the outcome includes trusting Him with the journey.
- The natural consequence of expectation is disappointment.
- Don't sit on your pity pot so long that you get a ring around your ass!
- Meditation is about being so in the moment that you can hear the Voice of God.
- Do you live your life thinking about solutions or complaining about the problems?
- Recovery is not a sentence; it is liberation.
- We get self-esteem by doing esteem-able things.
- It's not about what I get done today. It about how I exist in the process.
- It is not my thoughts, it's actions in response to thoughts that get us in trouble.
- Seldom when I give people a piece of my mind is it the better part.
- "Fix-oholics" try to make everything and everyone behave according to their plans.
- When someone is tripping out on life, remind them to look for the film crew following them.
- Triple Stupid = I don't know what I don't know. What I know isn't worth knowing. Everything I thought I knew was wrong.
- I love to make decisions. What I don't like is being responsible for the decisions I made.
- There is a price and a prize to every decision, even lack of decision. Is the prize worth the price?

- When the pain of change is exceeded by the change of staying the same, you will change.
- Life goes well if I let it.
- It doesn't matter how right I am. It matters what is right.
- Just because you can, doesn't mean you should.
- Do you want to be right--or to be happy?
- If I don't get what I want, it's because I am not ready to receive it.
- What happens in vagueness, stays in vagueness. - Debtors Anonymous
- Do the activities that will lead to your success, day after week after month after year.
- The stop sign is a whole lot better than ICU.
- I thank God for taking care of me and for not giving me what I deserve.
- After I become aware of what drives my behaviors, I can change the behaviors.
- Today I can sit in my feelings and know they won't kill me.
- I am not behind or ahead. I am doing the best I can today. I am right where I am supposed to be.
- I am reading the story. I am not writing it.
- What the caterpillar calls the end of the world, the Master calls a butterfly.
- Learn from your history. Never forget it. But don't live in it.
- I have a superpower to be so present that the Great I Am floods me with joy, peace, and gratitude.
- I am certain there is a God who has a plan for me to prosper, and I am certain I will!

- We argue the exception for ourselves because even a broken clock is right twice a day.
- If you are a raisin, you cannot be a grape. Self-delusion is bondage.
- Surrender = I am on duty, but I am not in charge.
- When we are open and aware that God is running the show, we see God running the show.
- It's not what I pick up (regarding knowledge), it's what I let go.
- Escaping into addiction means you cut off the pain. But numbness also cuts off the joy.
- Acceptance does not necessarily mean approval.
- If you fear the "pain" of moving forward, you will stay in the pain you no longer want.
- There is no law against a bad day.
- God will find you even if you are not seeking, even if you do not care to be found.
- I may not understand how you feel, but I am concerned about how you feel.
- You are not responsible for your disease. You are responsible for your recovery.
- God loves me so much He lets me be responsible for my words and actions.
- Make note of the daily miracles. Write them down! Don't just think, "A miracle!" Make note!
- Miracles happen all the time.
- Hope is a desire with expectation of fulfillment.
- God disciplines me by giving me what I wish for.
- True hope is the belief that it will all work out the way God wants--even better than we can dream.

- Definition of an addict = having normal people problems and choosing absurd solutions.
- They only have 10 rules and I am pretty sure I broke all those 10 and maybe a few more.
- I can be whoever and do whatever as long as it reflects love and service.
- When you ask for forgiveness from the past, receive it! Let the past remain the past.
- There is such a thing as the problem of prosperity, the problems related to our luxury.
- I had all these feelings, but I didn't have a reason for them. Time to let go and let God.
- I can't stay clean off of yesterday's shower.
- A child can accept responsibility. An adult accepts accountability.
- I figured it was mind over matter. Eventually, I didn't mind and you didn't matter.
- Act your way into right thinking. Even if you still think like a thug, act otherwise.
- Information helps us, but it does not save our ass.
- I am quite willing to suffer for my sins, but I don't want to correct them.
- I care about what happens to you as long as I don't have to get up off my ass and do anything.
- This was the problem with my life. I never really had to pay the consequences…until I did.
- I had book sense but didn't have relationship sense.
- Functional alcoholics can hold down jobs and don't use substances continually.
- Wrong became right. That became my natural.

- My natural tendency is to want to change the way I feel.
- When expectations turn into demands, you have to put in more than you ask for.
- I always wanted to lead the charge, but I had no idea where the enemy was.
- My spirituality is in my feet
- We had to lose to know how to win.
- Don't allow guilt and self-loathing stop you from growing and maturing.
- When you think something negative, say something positive to change your thoughts.
- Recovery is not for people who need it or want it. It's for people who will do it.
- Sorrow shared is sorrow diminished. Joy shared is joy expanded.
- A "normal" person changes their actions to meet their goals. An addict changes their goals.
- Your disease might be the dog's nose and my disease might be the dogs butt, but you know where the nose ends up. Don't be so high and mighty about where you start.
- This program isn't about me doing no harm, it's about can I be a better me, so I can better serve you.
- Spirituality is an action not a feeling.
- Peace, joy, success, and freedom are not for people who want it. It is for people who will work for it.
- Being unhappy about what is happening in the world doesn't help anyone.
- The reward is in the seeking, not the getting.

- I don't work on problems. I work on myself and the problems take care of themselves.
- Self-importance is like a naked man holding a barrel. You have to stay focused on yourself.
- If you are going to stir the shitpot, then ya gotta lick the spoon.
- You have to stop defending yourself in order to allow for what you will become.
- We are afraid of the wrong things.
- When I get into fear, it is because I am not giving God credit for what He's done for me in the past.
- I have transformed from a flawed person to a person with flaws.
- God does not close one door without opening another, but sometimes it is hell in the hallway.
- It takes a wise man to learn from the mistakes of others.
- I see things as I am, not as they are.
- What if I humbled myself--and nobody noticed?!
- God wants us to be happy, joyous and free. I confused this with rich, powerful, and famous.
- We can't open up the gates of heaven, but we can unlock the gates of hell.
- Would I hire myself to manage my life?
- Our world is full of very social people who don't really like anyone.
- Move a muscle, change a thought.
- A situation that is not to my liking may be a situation that is not to my understanding.
- The pain-to-joy ratio is wide for some. Some people don't have a basement.

- I can get someone to co-sign my denial fast.
- When I don't keep in daily contact with God, I get my thank you's and f you's mixed up.
- I am aware now that I have expected more from the universe than I contributed.
- There is no place to be. There is no one to become.
- The only thing I need to know about God is that I am not It.
- The more I stop trying to define God or telling Him who he is, the more I grow in my faith.
- I didn't expect to be in my 50s before I grew out of my teens.
- I am glad I survived myself.
- If I think it, it does not mean it is real or true.
- My opinions of others are not facts. They are actually just feelings which are subject to change.
- I am just doing what I am doing the best that I can.
- If you treat me special, I will feel okay. If you treat me normal, I will wonder why you don't like me.
- If it's a problem, and I can fix it, it ain't much of a problem.
- Be careful if you find yourself tuned into the radio station WIFM.
- You are exactly where you are supposed to be at the moment in the moment. Let it unfold.
- You have got to buy in for it to work. The power of belief is critical.
- It is imperative we serve others based on our ability and not based on our desires.

- Every time you find out who you are, you find out a little more of who you were.
- Four Roadblocks to spiritual growth:
    1 – Indifference - "I don't care."
    2 – Self-sufficiency/Isolation "I don't need you."
    3 – Prejudice - contempt before investigation "It won't work."
    4 – Defiance "Tell me what to do and I will tell you what I won't do."
- I didn't know there was a beginning or an end. I was just dealing with life moment by moment.
- Ego is like my bladder. You have to empty it several times, even a few times at night.
- Whenever it's my problem, it's a big deal. Whenever it's yours, it's not so difficult.
- At one point my life looked like a fairy tale but eventually it turned into a sad movie.
- It's not about getting what you want. It's about becoming who you are meant to be.
- I came to learn that the worst things that happened to me turned out to be some of the best things.
- Money is not math. Money is human behavior. - kvm
- It's not how much you make; it's how much you keep. - kvm
- Faith - Facts - Feelings. Order matters! - kvm
- Save 20. Pay Bills. Then Spend. Order Matters! - kvm
- The tragedy is what people think they know that just ain't so. - Will Rogers
- Hubris / Pride - If you think you are the exception, you WILL be the statistic. "

The principles Rabbi Sachs lays out for what is important in life:

1. Give thanks.
2. Give your children values, not presents.
3. Be a lifelong learner.
4. Never compromise your Judaism [your God] in public.
5. Forgive.
6. Don't talk lashon hara (evil speech- see below).
7. Keep Shabbat (rest – see below).
8. Volunteer.
9. Create moments of joy.
10. Love.

Rabbi Sachs defines "lashon hara": The Talmudic Sages define lashon hara, 'evil speech,' as saying negative things about other people even if they are true. They were harsh about it, regarding it as one of the worst interpersonal sins. Those who speak badly about others poison the atmosphere in families and communities. They undermine relationships and do great harm. They say, "But it's true," forgetting that lashon hara only applies to truth. If an allegation is false, it is called motsi shem ra ('spreading a bad name') and is a different kind of sin. They say, "But it's only words," forgetting that in Judaism words are holy, never to be taken lightly. See the good in people – and if you see the bad, be silent. **No one whose respect matters, respects those who speak badly of others.** http://rabbisacks.org/investing-time/ September 1, 2018

Rabbi Sachs defines "Shabbat": If Shabbat had not been created, someone would have made a fortune discovering and marketing it. Here is a one-day miracle vacation that has the power to strengthen a marriage, celebrate family, make you part of a community, rejoice in what you have rather than worrying about what you don't yet have, relieve you from the tyranny of smartphones, texts and 24/7 availability, reduce stress, banish the pressures of work and consumerism, and renew your appetite for life. It is supplied with wine, good food, fine words, great songs, and lovely rituals. You don't need to catch a plane or book in advance. It's a gift from God via Moshe, and for more than 3,000 years it has been the Jewish private island of happiness. To get there, all you need is self-control, the ability to say 'no' to work, shopping, cars, televisions, and phones. But then, everything worth having needs self-control. http://rabbisacks.org/investing-time/ September 1, 2018

MUSIC MAKES MERRY

Music affects our emotions (EQ) which shapes our thoughts (IQ). Further, the lyrics of music have a direct impact on our psyche. The God I follow makes it clear that we will be transformed by the renewal of our minds. What you read, what you listen to, what you watch, matter!

When you consider the body, 85% of health is about what you eat. Your exterior appearance, the aches and pains or lack thereof, is directly related to what you feed yourself. The mind, how you think and, therefore, how you feel, is no different. Your life is a reflection of what thoughts you entertain.

> Music is a source of creativity, especially when it's upbeat. When study participants listened to music labeled "happy," their creativity went up. The most effective music of all are songs with lyrics advocating kindness and helpfulness. Listening to positive lyrics can affect how kind and generous you will be and even how you'll spend your money. Positive song lyrics help make people less prejudiced and fearful of those different than them. Research confirms that the best type of music to increase focus and productivity should first and foremost be music you enjoy.[78]

Other research addresses how different types of music shape our personality such that while I might like the sound of gangsta rap, for example, lyrics which emphasize violence

---

[78] "How Music Affects the Brain," Deane Alban & Dr. Patrick Alban
https://bebrainfit.com/music-brain/

against authority, sexual domination of women, drugs, and alcohol, will not enhance my IQ and certainly not my EQ.

> The dark side of this is that lyrics can greatly influence the listener as well. Songs with negative lyrics or messages, when constantly listened to, becomes ingrained in a person's psyche and can be subconsciously recalled. So, it is also important to make sure lyrics are taken into consideration when listening to songs. Worship music alleviates emotional anxieties – sadness, depression, and a constantly negative personality can be alleviated by worship-music. Studies have shown that people who attend fellowships and engage in the listening and singing of worship music have improved levels of happiness and those with anxiety problems have felt improvements in their own personal feelings, after consistently attending and listening to the songs.[79]

As a tool to help my mind so I was more receptive to information (IQ) as well as enhance my ability to process my feelings (EQ), I chose to listen to what is called "worship" music because the words essentially affirm who I am, who God is, and what is all means as a whole.

Full disclosure, I detested worship music when I first started attending church regularly. As I was shopping for a spiritual home, if they sang too much during the service (and, please, do NOT raise your hands while singing!), I would leave. I chose to listen to "Christian" radio and participate in singing

---

[79] https://brainwavepowermusic.com/blog/blog/your-musical-taste-shows-and-affects-your-personality-and-behavior

during the church services not because I wanted to, but because I knew it was an action that if I practiced it enough, would transform my mind. I acted my way into right thinking and, viola, I am happier!

The following are songs that helped me and, as such, may they heighten your happiness! I have listed the songs and then provided some of the lyrics for a few of my favorites.

"Who You Say I Am" Hillsong Worship
"Known" Tauren Wells
"Surrounded" Michael W Smith
"You Say" Lauren Daigle
"Redeemed" Big Daddy Weave
"Fear is a Liar" Zach Williams
"What a Friend" Matt Maher
"More Than Anything" Natalie Grant
"Even If" Mercy Me
'O' Lord" Lauren Daigle
"Your Love Defends Me" Matt Maher
"No Longer Slaves" Bethel Music
"Holy Spirit" Francesca Battistelli
"All my hope is in Jesus" Crowder
"Chain breaker" Zach Williams
"Witness" Jordan Feliz

"Whole Heart" Brandon Heath
"The Breakup Song" Francesca Battistelli
"On your shoulders" Francesca Battistelli
"What A Beautiful Name" Hillsong Worship
"Same Power" Jeremy Camp
"Mighty To Save" Laura Story
"How Deep The Father's Love" Nichole Nordeman
"Counting Every Blessing" Rend Collective
"Broken Prayers" Riley Clemmons
"Confidence" Sanctus Real
"Come to the Table" Sidewalk Prophets

"Who You Say I Am" Hillsong Worship

Who am I that the highest King
Would welcome me
I was lost but He brought me in
Oh His love for me
Oh His love for me

Who the Son sets free
Oh is free indeed
I'm a child of God
Yes I am

Free at last
He has ransomed me
His grace runs deep
While I was a slave to sin
Jesus died for me
Yes He died for me

In my Father's house
There's a place for me
I'm a child of God
Yes I am

I am chosen
Not forsaken
I am who You say I am
You are for me
Not against me
I am who You say I am

"Known" Tauren Wells

It's so unusual it's frightening
You see right through the mess inside me
And you call me out to pull me in
You tell me I can start again
And I don't need to keep on hiding

(Chorus)
I'm fully known and loved by You
You won't let go no matter what I do
And it's not one or the other
It's hard truth and ridiculous grace
To be known fully known and loved by You
I'm fully known and loved by You

It's so like You to keep pursuing
It's so like me to go astray, ooh
But You guard my heart with Your truth
The kind of love that's bulletproof
And I surrender to Your kindness, oh
(Chorus)

How real, how wide
How rich, how high is Your heart
Now, I cannot find the reasons why
You give me so much
(Chorus)

"Surrounded" (Fight My Battles) Michael W Smith

This is how I fight my battles
It may look like I'm surrounded but I'm surrounded by You
This is how I fight my battles

"You Say" Lauren Daigle

I keep fighting voices in my mind that say I'm not enough
Every single lie that tells me I will never measure up
Am I more than just the sum of every high and every low?
Remind me once again just who I am, because I need to
know (ooh oh)

You say I am loved when I can't feel a thing
You say I am strong when I think I am weak
You say I am held when I am falling short
When I don't belong, oh You say that I am Yours
And I believe (I), oh I believe (I)
What You say of me (I)
I believe

The only thing that matters now is everything You think of
me
In You I find my worth, in You I find my identity, (ooh oh)
(Chorus)

Taking all I have and now I'm laying it at Your feet
You have every failure God, and You'll have every victory,
(ooh oh)
(Chorus)

"Redeemed" Big Daddy Weave

Seems like all I can see was the struggle
Haunted by ghosts that lived in my past
Bound up in shackles of all my failures
Wondering how long is this gonna last
Then You look at this prisoner and say to me "son
Stop fighting a fight that's already been won"
(Chorus)
I am redeemed, You set me free
So I'll shake off theses heavy chains
And wipe away every stain now I'm not who I used to be
I am redeemed
I'm redeemed

All my life I have been called unworthy
Named by the voice of my shame and regret
But when I hear You whisper, "Child lift up your head"
I remember oh God, You're not done with me yet
(Chorus)

Because I don't have to be the old man inside of me
'Cause his day is long dead and gone
Because I've got a new name, a new life I'm not the same
And a hope that will carry me home
(Chorus)

Oh God I'm not who I used to be
Jesus I'm not who I used to be

"Fear is a Liar" Zach Williams

When he told you you're not good enough
When he told you you're not right
When he told you you're not strong enough
To put up a good fight
When he told you you're not worthy
When he told you you're not loved
When he told you you're not beautiful
That you'll never be enough

Fear, he is a liar
He will take your breath
Stop you in your steps
Fear he is a liar
He will rob your rest
Steal your happiness
Cast your fear in the fire
'Cause fear he is a liar

When he told you were troubled
You'll forever be alone
When he told you you should run away
You'll never find a home
When he told you you were dirty
And you should be ashamed
When he told you you could be the one
That grace could never change

Let Your fire fall and cast out all my fears
Let Your fire fall Your love is all I feel

"What a Friend" Matt Maher

Everybody has trials and temptations
Everybody knows heart break, isolation
But we can lay our burdens down (our burdens down)
Lay our burdens down

(Chorus)
What a friend we have in Jesus
East to west my sins are gone
I see grace on every horizon
And forever and ever His heart is my home
Everybody has fears, everybody got worries
Everybody knows sorrow, devastation
But we can lay our burdens down (our burdens down)
Lay our burdens down
(Chorus)

"More Than Anything" Natalie Grant

I know if You wanted to You could wave Your hand
Spare me this heartache, and change Your plan
And I know any second You could take my pain away
But even if You don't, I pray

You know more than anyone that my flesh is weak
And You know I'd give anything for a remedy
And I'll ask a thousand more times to set me free today
Oh but even if You don't, I pray

Help me want the Healer
More than the healing
Help me want the Savior
More than the saving
Help me want the Giver
More than the giving
Oh help me want You Jesus
More than anything

"Even If" Mercy Me

They say sometimes you win some
Sometimes you lose some
And right now, right now I'm losing bad
I've stood on this stage night after night
Reminding the broken it'll be alright
But right now, oh right now I just can't

It's easy to sing
When there's nothing to bring me down
But what will I say
When I'm held to the flame
Like I am right now

I know You're able and I know You can
Save through the fire with Your mighty hand
But even if You don't
My hope is You alone

They say it only takes a little faith
To move a mountain
Well good thing
A little faith is all I have, right now
But God, when You choose
To leave mountains unmovable
Oh give me the strength to be able to sing
It is well with my soul

'O' Lord" Lauren Daigle

Though times it seems
Like I'm coming undone
This walk can often feel lonely
No matter what until this race is won
I will stand my ground where hope can be found

Oh, O Lord O Lord I know You hear my cry
Your love is lifting me above all the lies
No matter what I face this I know in time
You'll take all that is wrong and make it right

Your strength is found
At the end of my road
Your grace it reaches to the hurting
Still through the tears and the questioning why
I will stand my ground where hope can be found

"Your Love Defends Me" Matt Maher

You are my joy, You are my song
You are the well, the One I'm drawing from
You are my refuge, my whole life long
Where else would I go?

Surely my God is the strength of my soul
Your love defends me, Your love defends me
And when I feel like I'm all alone
Your love defends me, Your love defends me

Day after day, night after night
I will remember, You're with me in this fight
Although the battle, it rages on
The war already won
I know the war is already won

"No Longer Slaves" Bethel Music

You unravel me, with a melody
You surround me with a song
Of deliverance, from my enemies
Till all my fears have gone
I'm no longer a slave to fear
I am a child of God

From my mother's womb
You have chosen me
Love has called my name
I've been born again, into a family
Your blood flows through my veins
I'm no longer a slave to fear
I am a child of God

I am surrounded
By the arms of the father
I am surrounded
By songs of deliverance

We've been liberated
From our bondage
We're the sons and the daughters
Let us sing our freedom

You split the sea
So I could walk right through it
My fears were drowned in perfect love
You rescued me and I
Stand and sing
I am child of God

"Holy Spirit" Francesca Battistelli

There's nothing worth more
That could ever come close
No thing can compare
You're our living hope
Your presence, Lord
I've tasted and seen
Of the sweetest of loves
Where my heart becomes free
And my shame is undone
Your presence, Lord

Holy Spirit, You are welcome here
Come flood this place and fill the atmosphere
Your glory, God, is what our hearts long for
To be overcome by Your presence, Lord
Your presence, Lord

Let us become more aware of Your presence
Let us experience the glory of Your goodness

"All my hope is in Jesus" Crowder

I've been held by the Savior
I've felt fire from above
I've been down to the river
I ain't the same, a prodigal returned

(Chorus)
All my hope is in Jesus
Thank God that yesterday's gone
All my sins are forgiven
I've been washed by the blood

I'm no stranger to the prison
I've worn shackles and chains
But I've been freed and forgiven
And I'm not going back, I'll never be the same
That's why I sing
(Chorus)

There's a kind of thing that just breaks a man
Break him down to his knees
God, I've been broken more than a time or two
Yes, Lord then He picked me up and showed me
What it means to be a man
(Chorus)

"Chain breaker" Zach Williams

If you've been walking the same old road for miles and miles
If you've been hearing the same old voice tell the same old
lies
If you're trying to feel the same old holes inside
There's a better life

If you've got pain
He's a pain taker
If you feel lost
He's a way maker
If you need freedom or saving
He's a prison-shaking Savior
If you've got chains
He's a chain breaker

We've all search for the light of day in the dead of night
We've all found ourselves worn out from the same old fight
We've all run to things we know just ain't right
And there's a better life
There's a better life

If you believe it
If you receive it
If you can feel it
Somebody testify

"Witness" Jordan Feliz

I was blinded, you gave me eyes to see
I was going under, you reached out to me
No, there's nothing you won't do
To pick me up and pull me through
Every hour, eight days a week, yeah

(Chorus)
Your love is like a fountain
It'll never run dry, it'll never run dry
Your love is moving mountains
Every day of my life, every day of my life
Can I get a witness?
Oh, oh, oh, oh, hallelujah
Oh, oh, oh, oh, hallelujah

We want glory, but can't measure up
We try money, but don't get enough
We fill our sky with fainted lights
Try'n to guide us through the night
But you're the one thing, that'll carry us
(Chorus)

So much love, so much grace
C'mon now (can I get a witness?)
Somebody in this place
C'mon now (can I get a witness?)
So much love, so much grace
C'mon now (can I get a witness?)
Somebody in this place
C'mon now (can I get a witness?)
Ooh, ooh, ooh yeah(Chorus)

ABOUT THE AUTHOR

With decades of experience educating young adults to retirees and everyone in between, Kasandra Vitacca Mitchell has developed a formula for success that will enable one to achieve a desired outcome in any area of life – health, wealth, personal relations, spirituality, etc. On a daily basis, one will finally grasp the illusive "happiness" we all seek.

As a Financial Advisor for over a decade, Kasandra has helped thousands of people across America achieve financial security. Now, as a Speaker, Coach, and Author, she is on a mission to bring her research, wisdom, and authenticity to audiences as people implement "The Happiness Formula" into every area of their life.

Kasandra has an undergraduate degree and a Masters from Stanford University and after 15+ years as an "Organizational Design & Efficiency Expert" in corporate America, Kasandra has spent the last 10+ years as an Independent Financial Advisor specializing in insurance as an asset. She is based in Dallas/Fort Worth and serves clients around the nation.

She is a committed leader in the American Business Women's Association, a Leadership Coach with Texas Christian University BNSF Neely Leadership Program, and mentors women around the nation who want to increase their business acumen and/or their relationship with Yeshua. She is a philanthropist supporting many organizations and in 2018 created the "Vitacca-Mitchell Scholarship" to honor a student from her high school alma mater, Northview, in Covina, CA.

When she is not with her husband or adult children, she is at yoga, studying Hebrew and Torah, writing, reading, traveling, and discipling women as the Lord leads.

If you want success, wealth, and happiness, hire Kasandra to speak to your group today! www.kasandravitacca.com

The
Happiness
Formula

$$\underline{IQ + EQ + GQ = HQ^{TM}}$$

Kasandra Vitacca

Made in the USA
San Bernardino, CA
15 January 2019